Texas—Proud and Loud

By

BOYCE HOUSE

Illustrated by Winston Croslin

THE NAYLOR COMPANY
SAN ANTONIO, TEXAS

Other Books by the Same Author

I GIVE YOU TEXAS!
TALL TALK FROM TEXAS
OIL BOOM
WERE YOU IN RANGER?
TEXAS RHYTHM (Poetry)

To

a brilliant and dynamic Texan
whom Texas loaned to Tennessee . . .

JAMES LEONARD HIGHSAW

who, as high school teacher and debating coach,
imparted a lifelong inspiration

Acknowledgments

BESIDES individuals who are credited in the text of the book, grateful acknowledgment is made to C. D. Cannon, representing the George W. Saunders estate and to Marvin Hunter for Jack Potter's inimitable "Coming off the Trail"; to Donald Day and the Texas Folklore Society for "Injun Fight on the Llano" from "From Hell to Breakfast"; to Pfc. Ed Koops for "Pyote, Texas"; to many friends, including Judge Elzo Been, Bill Kittrell, Troy Simpson and Herschiel Hunt, as well as to the countless host of Texas talkers.

Table of Contents

Getting Started

TEXAS may be proud and loud, but then Texas has more to be proud about than any other State because — like the white horses eating more than the black horses — there is more of Texas than any other State.

More volunteers in World War II in proportion to population than any of her sister States —

More commissioned officers in the Army from Texas A. & M. than from any other institution —

The 36th Division, claimed as Texas' own, the first to invade the mainland of Europe —

Almost as much oil from Texas for the war effort as from all the other States put together —

A dozen Texas admirals, including Admiral Nimitz —

1

A hundred Texas generals, including General Ike Eisenhower —

These are just a few of the reasons that Texans have for their intense pride in their State.

Is it any wonder that the Axis hoped that Texas would grant a separate peace?

Texans loud? Why just suppose a Californian had half as much to talk about!

The Lone Star State, especially West Texas, is not far removed from the pioneering stage. If some of the stories that follow seem a bit crude, what would you expect of a region where the phrase that is "the first blow" in Kentucky is, when accompanied by a smile, simply a friendly, cow-country greeting — and where, moreover, that same Anglo-Saxon phrase has been bestowed upon a stew that is the most succulent and savory dish that can be found anywhere?

If it be asserted that a few of the tales are hyperbolic, so is the blue of the sky in this fantastic domain of twisted mesquite, giant cacti and horned frogs.

Incredible? So are the ceaseless wind, the boundless horizon and the forty-degree plunge of the temperature overnight.

Texas is the land where exaggerations are the truth.

Our State has known six flags and is the only one that won its own independence and was a republic all by itself. Explorers, treasure-seekers, pioneers, outlaws, two-gun officers, cowboys and oil men have given it a glamor that grows with the passing of time.

And so: First in cotton, first in cattle, first in petroleum, first in sheep, first in sulphur and first in Democrats — Texas, Proud and Loud!

Glorious
Texas

AN out-of-Stater said, "You Texans look down on other people, don't you?"

The rancher drawled, "Not that I know of — but we sure as h—— don't look up to anybody!"

☆　☆　☆　☆　☆　☆　☆

RECALLING the old saying of Sheridan that if he owned Texas and hell, he'd rent out Texas and live in hell, Don Weaver, editor of the Fort Worth Press, observes that wouldn't be a bad business proposition because, if the rent was only a dollar an acre, the general's income would be nearly $20,000 a day — and pretty soon, he'd be so rich that he could give hell to Hitler.

Or, with such an income (Weaver continued), the general could have hell air-conditioned and develop it as a tourist resort, "as there are bound to be a lot of interesting people there."

"Have you been here a long time?" the visitor asked a gray-haired settler in the Panhandle.

"A right smart while," the old-timer replied. "When I first come here, the moon was no bigger than a half dollar, and there was only six stars."

☆　☆　☆　☆　☆　☆　☆

In West Texas, there is a river a mile wide, a hundred miles long and four inches deep.

☆　☆　☆　☆　☆　☆　☆

In fact, in the middle of summer, this river has to be irrigated.

☆　☆　☆　☆　☆　☆　☆

An Englishman bought a ranch in West Texas and soon he and the cowboys were getting along fine.

"Fellows," he said, "we ought to get up a soccer team."

One asked, "How is it played?"

The Britisher explained, "You kick the ball, and if you can't kick the ball, you kick the fellow nearest you. I'll order the ball tonight, and we can start as soon as it gets here."

The exuberant cowhands yelled, "To h—— with the ball! Let's start now!"

☆　☆　☆　☆　☆　☆　☆

Even though they live on the border, some Texans know so little Spanish that they think manual labor is a Mexican.

☆　☆　☆　☆　☆　☆　☆

Pinto Pete died young but he left a lot of money behind; he was shot at 4 o'clock one morning as he was crawling out of the window of a bank.

☆　☆　☆　☆　☆　☆　☆

Of a ranchman whose holdings spread over half a dozen Texas counties, it was said: "He's no land hog; all the land he wants is just what joins his."

☆　☆　☆　☆　☆　☆　☆

A visitor comments that one of the chief characteristics of a Texan is that he makes no effort to conceal the disadvantageous points of the State — probably because he recognizes the impossibility of so huge an undertaking.

☆　☆　☆　☆　☆　☆　☆

An old-timer burned whole mesquite trees in the big fireplace. As the ends burned off, he kept moving the trees on into the flame. He explained, "It saves the old woman a lot o' choppin'."

☆　☆　☆　☆　☆　☆　☆

Before the days of the good neighbor policy, citizens of Mexico used to declare that their country could whip the United States if Texas would just keep out of the fight.

HE's an old Texas planter — an undertaker.

☆　☆　☆　☆　☆　☆　☆

THEN there was the Texan who was 17 years old before he found out that "durn yankee" was two words.

☆　☆　☆　☆　☆　☆　☆

A HUNTER in the Hill Country caught sight of a deer, but before he could fire, the animal had darted around a hill. Around and around that hill the hunter chased the deer but could never get a chance to shoot until he stopped, bent the rifle barrel across his knee to allow for the curvature of the hill and then fired, killing the creature, an eleven-point buck.

☆　☆　☆　☆　☆　☆　☆

A TRIP across vast Texas would make one of Mrs. Roosevelt's jaunts look like a walk to the corner drug store.

☆　☆　☆　☆　☆　☆　☆

A SIGN on the wall of a frontier Texas saloon read, "Don't shoot the piano player; he's doing the best he can."

☆　☆　☆　☆　☆　☆　☆

THE differing characteristics of three of the State's largest cities are said to be:
    When a traveling man has made a sale to a merchant—
    In Houston, the business man asks, "How soon can I get it?";
    In Dallas, "How much discount do I get?";
    In Fort Worth, "How long have I got to pay for it?"

☆　☆　☆　☆　☆　☆　☆

IT's so healthy out in West Texas that the Chamber of Commerce hired an Easterner to shoot himself so they could start a cemetery.

☆　☆　☆　☆　☆　☆　☆

THE difference between a yankee and a durnyankee is that the yankee has sense enough to stay where he belongs.

☆　☆　☆　☆　☆　☆　☆

SANTA ANNA MOUNTAIN so dominates the landscape that it was a landmark in early days in West Texas. Really, it is two mountains, there being a gap. Citizens explain that the town's original settler hauled in the dirt to build the mountain, and he would have connected it up, but his wagon broke down.

☆　☆　☆　☆　☆　☆　☆

THE Pecos River is famed for its twisting course. If you went from Pecos, Texas, to Carlsbad, N. M., by highway, it would be less than a hundred miles, but if you went by river, you'd travel seven times as far. The Forty-Niners are responsible, according to legend.
    They were in such haste to get to the California gold fields

that, when their wagons bogged in the Pecos, they would hitch an extraordinary number of oxen to a wagon and these oxen, giving one tremendous pull all at the same time, not only would bring the wagon out on the other bank but would also yank a big crook in the river-bed.

Yes, oxen in those days were mighty powerful.

☆   ☆   ☆   ☆   ☆   ☆   ☆

THE renowned description of the gigantic Texas steer stirred Edward M. Edwards to this rhapsody on his state's most famous product:

"If all our Missouri mules were made into one, he could rub his ears against the North Pole, with his forefeet on the Aleutians and Iceland, one hind foot on Havana and the other on Panama; and, if he got riled, he could kick South America 73 miles beyond the South Pole; his hee-haw would make a California earthquake sound like the rumble of one of Henry Ford's old puddle-jumpers; and, if he was properly hitched, he could pull Texas into the Republican Party."

☆   ☆   ☆   ☆   ☆   ☆   ☆

IN EARLY TIMES, a bunch got to talking about why each had come to Texas.

One had killed a man; another had held up a train; another had been accused of marrying four times without getting a divorce. When it came the last man's turn, he said:

"Well, boys, I came to Texas for something I didn't do."

At the general clamor of disbelief, he raised a hand for quiet and then continued:

"Back in Alabama, they raised $3,000 to build a church, and I was chairman of the finance committee, and I came to Texas for not building the church."

☆   ☆   ☆   ☆   ☆   ☆   ☆

WARRANT OFFICER JAMES V. LOVELL, who before the war was dramatic editor of the Dallas Times-Herald, quotes an out-of-State soldier as saying:

"The Army prepared guide books for every country in the world — and then sent us down to Texas without even a hint."

☆   ☆   ☆   ☆   ☆   ☆   ☆

LOVELL says that another trainee in the Lone Star State declared, "I'm used to flag-waving but Texans are the only people who wave six at the same time."

Git Along, Little Dogies

A CITY FELLER was spending the night in a shanty out on the range — just he and Handlebar Zeb. After supper, the talk turned to ghosts and they exchanged vivid tales. They had turned in — they bunked together on a pallet — and were just about to fall asleep when there came a queer sound.

The visitor whispered, "Zeb, did you hear that?"

"Yes, it might be a ghost," the other whispered as he raised himself stealthily, struck a match, then blew it out, stretched back out and remarked:

"Twasn't nothin' but an ole rattlesnake."

☆   ☆   ☆   ☆   ☆   ☆   ☆

"Who is the stranger?" a cowboy asked another.

"I dunno," his friend replied, "but he ain't no lawyer — he's got his hands in his own pockets."

"WHAT is the chief use of cowhide?" the teacher asked.

"To hold the cow together," answered little Henry.

☆ ☆ ☆ ☆ ☆ ☆ ☆

A MOTORIST, seeing a vaquero, stopped his car and engaged him in conversation.

"What do you cowpunchers do?" asked the motorist.

The Mexican cowboy told him:

"Three monts post hole dig and the fence feex. Three monts mule plow. Two monts alfalfa make. Two monts wood cut. Two monts hay pitch. Two weeks cow punch."

☆ ☆ ☆ ☆ ☆ ☆ ☆

"LITTLE excitement here a few minutes ago; Pistol Pete shot up the town and terrified a dude," said one native to another, just in from the ranch.

"Did the tenderfoot run?"

"Did he run?" the other repeated the question. "Why, he left town so fast his vest pocket was dippin' up sand."

☆ ☆ ☆ ☆ ☆ ☆ ☆

TWO COWBOYS were having a meal in town. One said, "The butter is so strong it could walk around the place and say hello to the coffee."

His friend said, "Well, if it did, the coffee is too weak to answer back."

☆ ☆ ☆ ☆ ☆ ☆ ☆

BRONCHO CHARLIE had had a big time in town, and now he reeled into the wagon yard and crawled under a wagon and went to sleep. The night was extremely cold, so a friend roused him and urged:

"Charlie, come inside; you'll freeze out here."

But the sleepy cowboy mumbled, "Naw — jes' throw another wagon over me for cover."

☆ ☆ ☆ ☆ ☆ ☆ ☆

A TENDERFOOT was up at the bar when three cowboys rode their horses into the saloon. He complained to the bartender, "These horses are jostling me." The bartender said, angrily, "What in thunder are you doin' in here on foot, anyhow?"

☆ ☆ ☆ ☆ ☆ .☆ ☆

"WHAT happened to that feller from the East that was visitin' the ranch?" the storekeeper asked a group of cowboys who were in town for a festive Saturday.

"Well," Chaparral Sid replied, "it was mighty sad. The very fust mornin' he was a-brushin' his teeth with some fancy tooth-paste and Zach here, seein' him a-foamin' at the mouth, thought he had hydrophoby an' killed him. Yep, it was mighty sad."

AN EASTERNER had come out to Texas to serve as the railroad agent in a little western town. One day, he received an invoice which called for "1 burro." He was not acquainted with the little donkeys that are seen in considerable numbers in the southern part of the State, so he reported to the main office of the railroad:

"Short, 1 bureau; over, 1 jackass."

☆　☆　☆　☆　☆　☆　☆

THE cowboy's horse lost his footing as he was traveling along the canyon trail and they plunged into space. Horse and rider had fallen 200 feet and were near the bottom when the cowboy showed presence of mind by jumping off. The fall, of course, killed the horse, but the rider had a drop of only twelve feet and was unhurt.

☆　☆　☆　☆　☆　☆　☆

THE tenderfoot had just taken his first horseback ride. "I didn't know anything filled with hay could be so hard," he moaned.

☆　☆　☆　☆　☆　☆　☆

A COWBOY was visiting in Los Angeles and, happening to read that a studio needed cowboys for a Western picture, applied. The director asked, "Are you a tenor or a baritone?"

"I can't sing," the Texan replied, "but I can ride any horse you've got."

"Do you play the guitar or the banjo?" the director inquired.

"No, but I won top money in the roping contest at the Fort Worth Fat Stock Show," was the reply.

"You're a h—— of a cowboy," the movie executive said. "Here, Jim, throw this imposter out."

☆　☆　☆　☆　☆　☆　☆

IT IS related of the great cattle king, Tom Waggoner, that when he was a young man, a committee was raising money to buy uniforms and instruments for the Vernon town band and young Tom subscribed $500.

When his father, Dan Waggoner, was solicited for a contribution, he said, "Put me down for $50."

The committee member protested, "But, Mr. Waggoner, your son gave $500."

"Yes," the old ranchman replied, "but then Tom has got a rich father; I ain't."

☆　☆　☆　☆　☆　☆　☆

TWO COWBOYS in the city were celebrating, and in the course of the evening met a friendly stranger. The trio visited several bars and were en route to another when their companion was seized with a heart attack in the street and fell dead.

Their senses somewhat blurred, the cowpunchers decided not

to abandon him, so, lifting him up, they took him, one by each arm, and walked into a saloon.

"Three whiskeys," one of them said as the bartender turned around.

The drinks had been placed in front of them when there was a commotion outside, and the cowboys, leaving their comrade slouched over the bar, went to see what the noise was.

The bartender remarked to the remaining customer, "How about paying for those drinks?"

When there was no reply, he said, "Oh, a smart guy, eh? Won't talk," and rapped him over the head with a bung-starter.

The body toppled over just as the cowboys re-entered. One looked at the inert form and said, "You've killed him."

The bartender, pale and trembling, said, "The son-of-a-gun drew a knife on me."

☆ ☆ ☆ ☆ ☆ ☆ ☆

THE cowboy had been drinking a little before he got on the bus, and, when he awoke from a nap, he said, "Hurray fer Texas!"

A passenger, whose home was in small Connecticut and who was weary from the interminable travel across Texas, snorted, "Hurray for h——!"

The cowpuncher said, "That's right; every man for his own country."

☆ ☆ ☆ ☆ ☆ ☆ ☆

AN OLD-TIME circuit-riding preacher liked his food highly seasoned, and so he carried around a bottle of tabasco sauce. A cowboy, seeing him use it, asked to try it and poured a generous amount on a steak. He took a bite and his eyes watered and he almost choked.

In a little while, the cowboy asked, "Parson, you preach h——, don't you?"

"Yes, indeed."

"Well," the cowpuncher said, "you're the first preacher I ever saw that carried samples of it around."

☆ ☆ ☆ ☆ ☆ ☆ ☆

THE cow-camp cook announced, "For supper, I've got thousands of things to eat — beans."

☆ ☆ ☆ ☆ ☆ ☆ ☆

J. EVETTS HALEY, noted author-rancher, tells this one:

The foreman had been in the old cattleman's employ several years, so he decided it was time to ask for a raise in pay.

"But," the ranchman said, "I can't afford to pay you any more than you're getting now."

The foreman insisted, "But you can't get along without me."

His employer said, "Jack, s'pose you was to die; reckon I'd have to get along without you then."

"Well, yes," the other conceded, "I guess you would."

"Then," the ranch owner said, "from here on, I'm just goin' to consider that you're dead."

☆ ☆ ☆ ☆ ☆ ☆ ☆

THE pair of cowboys had been on the trail for two days with a herd of cattle. During that time neither men nor animals had had any water. At last, they caught sight of a small stream and the cattle dashed in. One of the cowboys had gone up a little way above them to drink when he noticed that his companion was scooping up a hatful of water where the animals had stirred it up.

"Come up here where it ain't so muddy," the first one called out.

"It don't matter," his comrade replied. "I'm gonna drink it all, anyhow."

☆ ☆ ☆ ☆ ☆ ☆ ☆

BLACK BILL had been drinking and he was in a fighting mood. In a loud voice, he proclaimed in the crowded saloon, "I can lick airy feller that lives in this town." This was received in silence so, after a moment, he announced, "I can whip airy man that lives in this county." There was more silence and then he bellowed, "I can lick airy feller that lives in West Texas."

At this, a cowboy arose from a table and said, "I live in West Texas and you can't whip me" — and, with two powerful wallops, stretched the boaster out in the sawdust.

He got up, shook his head to clear his brain and declared, "I jest tried to take in too much territory."

☆ ☆ ☆ ☆ ☆ ☆ ☆

DIFFERENT was the experience of the braggart who entered a saloon with a piece of paper in his hand. In reply to a question, he said, "It's a list of the men I can whip."

"Is my name on there?" demanded a broad-shouldered ranchman.

"Yes."

"Well, you can't whip me."

"Are you right sure?"

"I sure am."

"Very well," replied the other, "I'll take your name off."

☆ ☆ ☆ ☆ ☆ ☆ ☆

PECOS BILL, the greatest of all cowboys, encountered the biggest of rattlesnakes, gave the rattler the first three bites and then subdued him. A little later, he met a huge mountain lion — the

one for whom the state of Nuevo Leon in Mexico was named —
and he had no trouble in overpowering the creature with his
bare hands. Then Pecos Bill climbed on the lion, spurred him
in the sides and, using the live snake as a quirt, rode into the
camp of the most notorious outlaws of the Southwest.

"Who's the boss here?" he demanded.

A fellow arose; he had on five six-shooters and four Bowie
knives. He said:

"I was, but you are now."

☆   ☆   ☆   ☆   ☆   ☆   ☆

IN HIS spare time, Pecos Bill amused himself by putting the horns
on toads and the thorns on the cacti.

He invented the tarantula and the centipede as a joke on
his friends; and he dug the Rio Grande when he got tired of
packing water from the Gulf of Mexico.

Pecos Bill is the man who staked out New Mexico; and as for
Arizona, why he used it for a pasture.

☆   ☆   ☆   ☆   ☆   ☆   ☆

THE great love of Pecos Bill's life was Slue-foot Sal. He saw her
riding a catfish down the Rio Grande, using only a surcingle,
and it was love at first sight.

But because Slue-foot Sal was a great rider, it was to cause
her death. On the wedding day, she insisted on riding her sweet-
heart's fiery horse, Widow-Maker. At the very first jump, Slue-
foot Sal was flung high in the air. Now she was wearing her
wedding raiment, including a steel spring bustle, and when she
hit the ground she bounced up as high as she had been, and this
bouncing kept up, hour after hour, for three whole days and at
last Pecos Bill had to shoot his bouncing bride to save her from
a lingering death by starvation.

☆   ☆   ☆   ☆   ☆   ☆   ☆

THE mightiest of the cowboys was chivalrous — he never killed a
woman (except the mercy slaying of Slue-foot Sal), nor a child
— nor a tourist, out of season.

Pecos Bill was so tough that not even Somervell County
likker had any "kick" to him, so he took to strengthening it with
fish-hooks and barbed wire — and that's what caused his death;
his stomach rusted.

☆   ☆   ☆   ☆   ☆   ☆   ☆

ANOTHER version is that his death was caused by an Easterner
rigged up in a mail order cowboy outfit. When Pecos Bill caught
sight of him, he laughed himself to death.

In the Back-woods

A BIG army camp was established over in the hills of East Texas near the Arkansas and Louisiana lines. One day, as an old settler was riding along the road on his mare, he saw soldiers approaching on foot and he turned aside to let them pass. But on and on came more and more men; it seemed that the lines would never end.

At last, the old man took off his hat and yelled, "Hurray, boys! You'll lick them d—— Yankees this time."

☆　☆　☆　☆　☆　☆　☆

THE farmer was in town for a little Saturday buying and the storekeeper asked, "Well, what did you name your new son?"

"Can't name him till one o' the dogs dies," the man replied; "the dogs got all the good names."

Sɪ's ʜᴏʀsᴇ was sick but so was the veterinarian, and he was unable to go out to the farm and view the animal. "I'll just fix up some medicine for you to give the horse," he said.

"How will I give it?" Si wanted to know.

"That's simple; just put the medicine in a tube, put the tube in the horse's mouth, and blow," the veterinarian directed.

A week later, he saw Si, who looked pale and weak, and the farmer explained, "That hoss like to a-ruined me; he blowed fust."

☆　☆　☆　☆　☆　☆　☆

Fᴀʀᴍᴇʀ Pᴇʀᴋɪɴs had never seen an electric fan and he gazed in fascination at the one in operation in the bank. He stood around a long time and the president asked if there was anything he could do for him. The farmer replied:

"No, I jes' want to see the squirrel that turns that cage so fast."

☆　☆　☆　☆　☆　☆　☆

Tʜᴇ customer asked the waitress in a small town cafe, "What kind of pie do you have?"

She replied, "Open, lattice an' kivered — but it's all apple."

☆　☆　☆　☆　☆　☆　☆

Iɴ ᴛʜᴇ early days of the automobile in Texas, the law required that when a motorist·met a horse and buggy or a wagon, he must stop and, if necessary, get out and help lead the animals past.

Hiram and Samantha had never seen an auto and suddenly they saw and heard a roaring monster coming toward their wagon.

The driver got out and said, "Can I help you get your mules past?"

The farmer replied, "The mules are all right; you help me git the old woman by."

☆　☆　☆　☆　☆　☆　☆

Tʜᴇ backwoods wife visited the village doctor with a double mission, for both her husband and the horse were sick. After the physician had prepared two bottles, she said:

"Be shore an' write plain which is fer the hoss and which is fer my ole man; I don't want nothin' to happen to the hoss afore spring plowin'."

☆　☆　☆　☆　☆　☆　☆

"Hᴀᴠᴇ I lived here very long!" the elderly whittler exclaimed. "Why, when I fust come here, thar was only one other settler in the county and that hill you see over thar was a buffalo waller."

Do YOU remember when garages used to display a sign: "Automobiles repaired; Fords fixed"?

☆   ☆   ☆   ☆   ☆   ☆   ☆

THAT was back in the days of the Model T ("a rattling good car") — and you still see some of those old-timers chugging along the roads in parts of East Texas. At sight of these twenty-year-old models, one is reminded of the rash of Ford jokes, such as the one about the man who drove a particularly battered roadster into a filling station and the attendant said:

"Want me to jack up the radiator cap and run in a good car under it?"

☆   ☆   ☆   ☆   ☆   ☆   ☆

AND the one about the man who wrote to the Ford plant, "I understand recently you made a complete car in five minutes." When a letter came back that this was correct, he wrote again, "I got it."

☆   ☆   ☆   ☆   ☆   ☆   ☆

IT WAS his brother whose barn was hit by a tornado and the tin roof was ripped off. He bundled up the debris and shipped it to the Ford factory. A few weeks later, he received a note, "We have repaired your car and are shipping it to you today. Pardon us for saying so, but it was the worst-wrecked Ford we ever saw."

☆   ☆   ☆   ☆   ☆   ☆   ☆

AND one farmer said he wanted his flivver buried with him, explaining: "I never saw the hole that my ole tin Lizzie couldn't get me out of."

☆   ☆   ☆   ☆   ☆   ☆   ☆

A MAN driving a wheezy jalopy was halted by a toll-bridge keeper, who said:

"Fifty cents."

The man jumped out of the car and said:

"Sold!"

☆   ☆   ☆   ☆   ☆   ☆   ☆

THEY were raising money to repair the church and a committee member called on Uncle Walt.

"Can't give nothin'," he said.

"But," the solicitor insisted, "you owe more to the Lord than you do to anybody."

"Yes, that's so," Uncle Walt replied, "but He ain't pushin' me like my other creditors are."

☆   ☆   ☆   ☆   ☆   ☆   ☆

"HUCK was a-runnin' you down jes' now," a villager said. "He declared you wasn't fitten to associate with the hogs. But I took up fer you — I said you was."

THE first World War had begun and a group was talking about it in the "hill country" store, when Hank rode up. He lived the fartherest back in the hills, and this was before the days of radio, of course.

The merchant greeted him with, "Hank, Germany has invaded Belgium; France has declared war on Germany, and so have England and Russia; and Austria has come in on the other side; great battles are raging; in fact, it is the biggest war in the history of the world."

He paused and everyone waited to see what Hank's comment would be. He felt all eyes upon him and knew that he was called upon to say something. At last, he remarked:

"Well, they got a purty day fer it."

☆　☆　☆　☆　☆　☆　☆

THEY had been married twenty-five years when the wife became ill and breathed her last. As the coffin was being carried through the front gate, one of the pallbearers slipped and the corner of the coffin struck the gate-post. There was a sigh from the "corpse" and she sat up. She had not been dead but only in a profound coma.

Several years went by and the woman became ill and died. As the coffin was being carried out the gate for the second time, the bereaved husband said, "Watch out for that post, boys."

☆　☆　☆　☆　☆　☆　☆

"ON THAT last great day," the evangelist shouted, "there will be weeping and wailing and gnashing of teeth!"

"But," broke in Sister Spraggins, "I haven't got no teeth!"

"Silence, Sister," the preacher said, "teeth will be provided."

☆　☆　☆　☆　☆　☆　☆

"HURRY down to the big road an' help my paw," said the little boy as he ran up to a cabin door.

"What's happened?" the settler wanted to know.

"He fell off the wagon into the mud."

"Is he in very deep?"

"He's plumb up to his ankles."

"Oh, well, he's not bad off then."

"Yes, mister," the boy said, "but he fell in head fust."

☆　☆　☆　☆　☆　☆　☆

BACK in prohibition days, a carnival came to town. A few hours later, there was a great commotion — the fire-eater drank some corn-likker and nearly burnt up!

☆　☆　☆　☆　☆　☆　☆

IN THAT section, they used to estimate the corn crop not as so many bushels, but so many gallons, per acre.

SIXTEEN-YEAR-OLD HANK proudly announced at the supper-table, "I made a hundred in arithmetic today. The teacher asked how much was thirty and twenty and I said forty-two."

His mother spoke up, doubtfully, "Is that right?"

"Naw, maw, but I was closer than any of the others in the class."

☆ ☆ ☆ ☆ ☆ ☆ ☆

THE old couple had been married nearly 50 years. Then she began reading "Hints on Manners" in the ready-print section of the county paper and tried to improve her husband's etiquette, but without success.

Finally, one morning at breakfast, she said, "Hiram, ef you don't quit drinkin' coffee outen the saucer, I'll leave you."

He looked across the table in stunned silence for a full minute and then he replied, "Honey, I'm gonna miss you."

☆ ☆ ☆ ☆ ☆ ☆ ☆

OVERTAKEN by a heavy rain that made the country road impassable, a motorist asked shelter for the night at a cabin in the piney woods. Next morning, he was out on the back porch where, after brushing his teeth and combing his hair, he lathered his face, shaved, and then dusted talcum powder over his features. The youngest boy in the family was an interested spectator throughout and at last he spoke up:

"Mister, air you that much trouble to yourself every mornin'?"

☆ ☆ ☆ ☆ ☆ ☆ ☆

SI DECIDED to visit the city for the first time and he took his wife and eight sons and six daughters, too. He was strolling along the main street when a policeman came up and said to him, "You are under arrest."

The astonished farmer asked, "What have I done?"

The officer said, "I don't know — but if you haven't done something, what's all this crowd following you for?"

☆ ☆ ☆ ☆ ☆ ☆ ☆

THE crossroads community had never heard tell of an automobile, and the group on the porch of the general store stared in amazement as a car roared by and disappeared over the hill.

"Whut in tarnation wuz that darn thing?" one demanded.

Just then around the bend there came in view a motorcycle.

"Don't know," replied another, "but here comes its colt."

☆ ☆ ☆ ☆ ☆ ☆ ☆

FARMER JENKS' horse has a lot of good points; in fact, you could hang your hat on some of them.

AND when his owner is riding him, this horse is so afraid that
the farmer will say "Whoa!" and he won't hear him that he
stops every once in a while and listens.

☆   ☆   ☆   ☆   ☆   ☆   ☆

A LANKY INDIVIDUAL sat in the doorway of his cabin over in the
region close to the Louisiana line.

"What do you raise?" asked a motorist, who stopped for a
chat.

"Hogs."

"What else?"

"That's all — just hogs."

"Why do you raise nothing but hogs?" the tourist inquired.

"Hogs don't need no plowin'," the native replied.

☆   ☆   ☆   ☆   ☆   ☆   ☆

HE MUST have been a neighbor to the farmer, who was asked
by a tourist:

"Going to raise some corn?"

"Naw — didn't plant no corn: afeered of the corn-borer."

"Then you are going to raise some cotton?"

"Naw — boll weevil too bad."

"Oats, maybe?"

"Naw — skeered dry weather would ruin 'em."

"Then," the traveler asked, "what did you plant?"

"Didn't take no chances; didn't plant nothin'," was the reply.

☆   ☆   ☆   ☆   ☆   ☆   ☆

Two little boys were looking at the man lying in the gutter. One
said, "He shore is drunk."

The other remarked, "Naw, he ain't; I jes' seen him wiggle
his little finger."

☆   ☆   ☆   ☆   ☆   ☆   ☆

WHEN Farmer Smithers passed away, he left a little property,
and his three boys went into the county seat to probate the will.
There was some delay and they had to make several trips, and
still the matter had not been concluded. As they loaded into
the wagon for the fourth journey into town, Joe, the oldest son,
remarked:

"Boys, ef this keeps up much longer, durned ef I won't
almost be sorry the ole man died."

☆   ☆   ☆   ☆   ☆   ☆   ☆

IT WAS decided to beautify the cemetery and so a committee set
out to raise funds to build a fence around it. But when a committee member called on Horace Hardscrabble, he said, "Nope,
'taint needed; those on the outside don't want to git in and
those on the inside cain't git out."

TWO MEN met in town and one asked, "Did you tell George Hankins that I was a liar?"

The other replied, "Naw, he musta found it out from somebody else."

☆　☆　☆　☆　☆　☆　☆

THE traveling salesman driving through the hills slammed on the brakes with amazement at the sight before him: an old man, with gray whiskers down to his waist, out in the middle of the road, crying.

"What in the world is the matter?" the traveler asked.

"Paw spanked me," was the reply.

"Your father spanked you? For goodness' sake, what for?"

"For throwin' rocks at gran'pappy," the old man sobbed.

☆　☆　☆　☆　☆　☆　☆

THE two rural youths were taking their first train ride. The news butch came through with the soda pop and each bought a bottle.

Jeff took a swallow and just then the train entered a tunnel. He yelled, "Pete, don't you drink that stuff; I've been struck blind!"

☆　☆　☆　☆　☆　☆　☆

A SETTLER from the hills, hearing that a new teacher had come into the community and opened up a school, brought in his boy, Jim, and demanded:

"Whut kin you teach?"

The teacher replied, "I can teach Latin, grammar, French, geography, arithmetic, geometry, trigonometry——"

"That's it," the father broke in, "triggernometry! Jim's the only poor shot in the family!"

☆　☆　☆　☆　☆　☆　☆

IT WAS early in the history of motion pictures and the first film ever seen was being shown in the town. It was a one-reeler, showing a group of young women on a street car. They alighted at a stretch of the beach and began disrobing—but at that point a freight train came along, and when it had passed, they were in their bathing suits.

Newt Brown sat through six performances of the new marvel, and when at last he came out, he said, "That durn train was right on time every time."

☆　☆　☆　☆　☆　☆　☆

THE first Arkansawyer to come to Texas ran across the boundary. He was following a Watkins man's buggy to see if the big wheels ever caught up with the little ones.

A NEW POSTMASTER was appointed for the little town. When three weeks had gone by and no mail had gone out from the place, an inspector was sent to investigate. He asked the postmaster for an explanation and that official said:

"Why, the sack ain't near full yet — you can see for yourself."

☆   ☆   ☆   ☆   ☆   ☆   ☆

HIRAM had never seen an automobile, much less a motorcycle, so when one of these latter came along the road, he grabbed his rifle and fired.

His wife said, "Did you git the varmint?"

"No," Hiram said, "I can still hear it but I shore made it turn that man loose."

☆   ☆   ☆   ☆   ☆   ☆   ☆

"How's yore paw?" one youth asked.

"He's gonna die," the other said, sadly.

"I wouldn't give up hope," the friend consoled.

"There ain't no chance fer him; the doctor says so — and he knows whut he give him," the son replied.

☆   ☆   ☆   ☆   ☆   ☆   ☆

GRANDPAPPY WITHERSPOON every morning took a gourdful of whiskey. When his ninety-seventh birthday was almost at hand, the old man passed away.

A neighbor gave the news to a visitor. The latter commented, "So whiskey finally got 'im, eh?"

☆   ☆   ☆   ☆   ☆   ☆   ☆

THE train had stopped to allow the passengers to eat. In front of one of the eating-places, a lank fellow stood, beating on a tray with a long-handled spoon. A flap-eared hound at his feet was howling. Without missing a lick on the tray with the spoon, the man looked down and said:

"What in thunder are YOU howling for? You don't have to eat the durned stuff!"

☆   ☆   ☆   ☆   ☆   ☆   ☆

THEN there was the old country boy who was taking his first train ride.

The news butch came through and the boy bought a banana. In a little while the butch returned and asked the lad if he wanted another.

"Naw," the young traveler said, "they're all right, but they got too much cob."

☆   ☆   ☆   ☆   ☆   ☆   ☆

IN ONE community it is said that when they find a man who can count up to twenty without taking off his shoes, they hire him to teach school.

"GOT a sick hoss over at my place," said one farmer to another.

"What seems to be the matter?"

The owner described the symptoms and then the other said, "I had a hoss sick like that a few weeks back and I give him a pint o' turpentine."

They did not meet for about a month, and when they did, the owner of the sick horse reported, "I give him that turpentine but he died."

"So did mine," said the other.

☆ ☆ ☆ ☆ ☆ ☆ ☆

A LITTLE BOY from the country was visiting his uncle, who, at the breakfast table, asked: "Joe, will you have some molasses?" The lad replied, "How kin I have mo' 'lasses when I ain't had no 'lasses yit?"

☆ ☆ ☆ ☆ ☆ ☆ ☆

A MAN drove up to a farmhouse and the farmer's wife came to the door. "I want to see your husband," he said. She answered, "Hiram's down at the barn, feedin' the mules; he's the one with his hat on."

☆ ☆ ☆ ☆ ☆ ☆ ☆

A CITY LAWYER was making a speech against a candidate for governor a good many years ago to a crowd in a little town. He sank his voice almost to a whisper, looked cautiously around, and said:

"There are no ladies present, I believe. My friends, that feller is a golfer!"

At the sinister-sounding word, the listeners looked from one to another in horror, and the box went solidly against him.

☆ ☆ ☆ ☆ ☆ ☆ ☆

THE hills are steep in parts of East Texas. A motorist, rounding a bend, slapped on his brakes just in time to keep from hitting a man who was sprawled in the middle of the road. The native got up and said, "Consarn! That's the third time this mornin' I've fell outta that field."

☆ ☆ ☆ ☆ ☆ ☆ ☆

A VISITOR asked the town's oldest inhabitant: "How long have you had that axe?"

The native said: "That axe is 75 years old — I bought it when I was a boy."

The visitor remarked: "Strange! It seems to be quite as good as new."

"Well," the old gentleman replied, "it's had three new blades and five new handles, but, excepting that, it's just the same — just the same."

A BUNCH of friends from Punkin Center set out to visit the city.

Arriving there at night, they engaged one big room at a hotel and decided to walk around and see the sights — all but Henry. For Henry had a supply of free postcards showing a picture of the hotel, and he wanted to send them to friends back home with the message: "Having fine time; wish you were here."

When he finished writing the cards, his friends hadn't returned, and, as he didn't want them waking him up to get in, he locked the door and threw the key through the transom into the hall, where he hoped the others would find it.

Next morning one of them said: "Henry, you locked yourself in. What if there had been a fire?"

"Oh," said Henry, "I wouldn't a-went."

☆   ☆   ☆   ☆   ☆   ☆   ☆

A VISITOR from the city remarked to a backwoodsman, "You say you use a straight-edged razor; don't you cut yourself pretty often?"

"Naw," the other replied, "I been shavin' with it for three year, and I didn't cut myself either time."

☆   ☆   ☆   ☆   ☆   ☆   ☆

THE farmer was dozing as he jogged along to town with a wagon-load of watermelons. When the vehicle hit a chug-hole, the endgate was jarred out and, going up the next hill, all the melons rolled out. Still the driver napped until, waking, he found team and wagon bogged down in a mud-hole. He glanced back and then exclaimed:

"Stuck, by gum, and not a durn thing to unload!"

☆   ☆   ☆   ☆   ☆   ☆   ☆

A FARMER was visiting the city for the first time.

He stood for an hour on a corner in the center of the big town watching the endless stream of trucks, buses and automobiles, and that night he wrote a postcard to the folks back home, saying: "They sure are behind in their hauling here."

☆   ☆   ☆   ☆   ☆   ☆   ☆

THE twin boys were fourteen years old and had never been to town. "Next Sattidy," the father said, "you can go in an' see the sights."

So they saddled their horses, rode in to the county seat, watched the horse-shoe pitching, drank two pink milk-shakes and were walking down the street when they saw a team rushing wildly toward them, the driver standing up, and shouting frantically.

"Pete," yelled one of the boys, "let's stop the runaway."

So they ran out, and one grabbed hold of the bridle of one

horse and the other boy seized the bridle of the other horse, dug the heels of their boots deep into the sand and, after a struggle, brought the team to a stop.

Then the boys, panting but grinning with pride, waited for praise from the crowd for having saved the driver's life.

To their amazement, that ungrateful individual yelled, "You durn fools, git outta the way—you've stopped the fire wagon on the way to a fire!"

☆　☆　☆　☆　☆　☆　☆

A MAN was telling a new friend how to find his house when he came for a visit. He said:

"You go a long ways down this road. You'll come to a red barn, but that's not me. Keep on going until you come to an old house, but that's not me either. Just keep on and you'll come to a white house with a pig in the yard — that's me."

☆　☆　☆　☆　☆　☆　☆

A TRAVELER jogging along on horseback heard a moaning sound, and as he rounded a turn, he saw the source — a native seated beside the road.

"What in the world is the matter?" the stranger asked.

The man stopped moaning long enough to reply, "I'm settin' on a sand-burr and it hurts like h——!"

☆　☆　☆　☆　☆　☆　☆

A STRANGER was attending a dance in Texas in pioneer days. After two or three dances, all the men suddenly drew their Bowie knives — and he shook with fright. But all they did was remove the splinters from the girls' feet.

☆　☆　☆　☆　☆　☆　☆

A BACKWOODSMAN was having a tooth filled. The dentist drilled a while, then tested the cavity with a little bulb and asked, "Do you feel that air?" The patient asked, "That air what?"

☆　☆　☆　☆　☆　☆　☆

A MOTORIST in the hill country was startled when a woman emerged from the woods so suddenly that he had to slap on his brakes to keep from running over her. She had scarcely disappeared on the other side of the road when here came a gangling youth in pursuit. The traveler jumped out and grabbed him, exclaiming: "This is outrageous!" The other explained, "Ah, shucks, mister; that's my maw and this is my seventeenth birthday and she's a-tryin' to wean me."

☆　☆　☆　☆　☆　☆　☆

THERE was one family that moved so often that, when they loaded the cook-stove onto the wagon, all the chickens lay down and stuck their legs up in the air to be tied.

THE tourist caught sight of a settler standing down near the road, and he had whiskers that swept almost to his knees. The motorist stopped his car and called out, "Old man, have you lived here all your life?"

The farmer shifted his chaw to the other jaw and drawled, "Not yit."

☆   ☆   ☆   ☆   ☆   ☆   ☆

THE twin boys were ten years old before they came in from the log cabin in the woods for their first visit to town. They looked at the sights, and then one turned to the other and said, "Bill, all the folks have got shoes on; it must be Sunday."

☆   ☆   ☆   ☆   ☆   ☆   ☆

GRANDPA WITHERSPOON was chatting with a group at the village store.

"What do you attribute your long life to?" one asked.

"I can't say yit," the patriarch replied; "there is several o' them testimonial fellers dickerin' with me."

☆   ☆   ☆   ☆   ☆   ☆   ☆

A MOTORIST bouncing along over a rough road stopped to ask a native, "Where does this road go?"

"Well, stranger, it just sorter plays out," the other replied.

"What do you mean by that?"

"Purty soon it gets to be jest a trail, then a hog-path, and after that it becomes a squirrel-track that goes up a hickory tree and winds up in a knot-hole!"

☆   ☆   ☆   ☆   ☆   ☆   ☆

TWO OLD LADIES who were neighbors had a falling-out. It came about because one asserted that the other had borrowed a pitcher and, when she returned it, the pitcher was cracked. The other woman was indignant:

"In the first place," she said, "I returned the pitcher to you in good condition.

"And in the second place, it was cracked when I borrowed it.

"And in the third place, I never borrowed it at all."

☆   ☆   ☆   ☆   ☆   ☆   ☆

BY WAY of entertaining visitors, the villagers used to offer Lem, the village half-wit, a dime or a penny, and he always chose the penny, which was the larger coin, of course.

One day, a visitor happened to be chatting with Lem off to one side and he asked, "Why do you always take the penny? Don't you know the dime is worth ten times as much?"

"O' course," Lem answered, "but ef I ever once took the dime, those durn fools would quit offerin' money to me."

IN THE rather early days of the automobile, an East Texas town began to be troubled by speeding, so a sign was posted, "Speed limit, 30 miles an hour." Farmer Corntassel, entering town in his buggy for the first time since the sign had been put up, read it and then exclaimed, as he applied the whip to his horse:

"Ole mare, reckon we kin make it?"

☆   ☆   ☆   ☆   ☆   ☆   ☆

AND IT was along about this time that two friends were en route to Tyler. They saw a sign, "Tyler, 20 miles." They drove for half an hour over the dirt road and then saw another sign, "Tyler, 20 miles." Another half hour passed and they came to a third sign, "Tyler, 20 miles."

One of the men turned to the other and said, "Thank goodness, we're holding our own."

☆   ☆   ☆   ☆   ☆   ☆   ☆

THE Punkin Center band was giving its first concert. At the conclusion of the opening number, somebody in the crowd called out, "Play Suwanee River." The director exclaimed, "Why, we just got through playing that!"

☆   ☆   ☆   ☆   ☆   ☆   ☆

IT WAS this same band that was performing one evening; the selection was "My Old Kentucky Home." The leader noticed a stranger in the crowd was crying, so at the conclusion of the number, he asked:

"My friend, are you a Kentuckian?"

"No," the stranger replied, "I'm a musician."

☆   ☆   ☆   ☆   ☆   ☆   ☆

THE "city fellow" hadn't the faintest idea where he was so when he overtook a lad, he brought the car to a halt and asked, "How far is it to Dallas?"

"Dunno," said the boy.

"Which way is Dallas, then?"

"Dunno."

"Well, where does this road go to?"

"Dunno."

Exasperated, the traveler said, "You don't know much, do you?"

"Naw," answered the boy, "but I ain't lost."

☆   ☆   ☆   ☆   ☆   ☆   ☆

A SIMILAR story:

A motorist, in need of directions, called out to a lad, "Jim, which way is Lufkin?"

"How did you know my name was Jim?" the boy asked.

"Oh, I just guessed it."

"Then guess which is the way to Lufkin," the youth said.

PERKINS was a smart trader; his friend, Billings, wasn't so smart. They bought a cow in partnership, Billings owning the front half and Perkins the rear half. Some weeks later, an acquaintance asked Billings how the deal was coming along and he answered:

"I was always having to feed my end of the cow and he got all the milk—so I quit feeding my half and his half died."

☆　☆　☆　☆　☆　☆　☆

THE old frontiersman had lived a free-and-easy life. But now, past 80, and so weak he had to take to his bed, he sent for the doctor.

"Doc," he inquired, "what do you think of this here death-bed repentance?"

"It's probably better than nothing at all," the physician replied.

"Well," the old fellow said, "ef I don't feel no better by mornin', durned ef I don't try it!"

☆　☆　☆　☆　☆　☆　☆

IT WAS during World War II and Farmer Jones had lost one hired man on account of the draft, and then another because of the lure of higher pay in a war industry. In desperation, he hired a stranger who actually was a "town feller" with no farming experience whatever. The first morning, the farmer roused his new employee. The dawn had not yet come, and the hired man asked, "What time is it?"

"Four o'clock," the farmer replied, "it's time to get up and start harvesting the oats."

"Are these oats wild?" the other persisted.

"No," the farmer answered.

"Then why do we have to slip up on them in the dark?"

☆　☆　☆　☆　☆　☆　☆

A VARIATION:

This time it was potatoes that the inexperienced hired man was awakened in order to harvest.

"Go get the fellow that planted them," the other yawned. "He knows where he put 'em."

☆　☆　☆　☆　☆　☆　☆

A SIMILAR story is the one about the miserly farmer who had a new hired man and the first morning for breakfast the employee devoured nine biscuits, five eggs and three pieces of ham.

The agitated employer said, "Why don't we just go ahead and eat dinner now?" The other agreed and proceeded to eat another egg and sop up three helpings of gravy.

The farmer, viewing this devastation in alarm, urged, "We

might as well eat supper, too, while we're at it." So the hired man ate one more biscuit with butter and pushed back his chair with a sigh of content.

"All right," the farmer said, "let's get busy with the milking."

"Oh, no," the other replied, "a man's time is his own after supper."

    ☆   ☆   ☆   ☆   ☆   ☆   ☆

IT MUST have been the same frugal farmer who awoke a new hired hand at the first streak of dawn with this admonition:

"Get up, get up; this is Monday; tomorrow's Tuesday; next day's Wednesday — half the week gone an' not a durn lick o' work done yet!"

    ☆   ☆   ☆   ☆   ☆   ★   ☆

A LAD called to a farmer who was in the yard, "I jes' had an accident; our wagon-load o' hay turned over in the road."

"Come in," said the farmer, kindly, "and have a glass o' lemonade."

"Paw wouldn't like it."

"Aw, he wouldn't mind" — and the cooling drink was pressed into the boy's hands.

After he had partaken of the lemonade, the hospitable farmer said, "Wife, set an extra plate at the table; it's about dinner-time."

The boy said, "Paw wouldn't like it."

But the farmer and his wife insisted and so he joined them at the table. After the hearty meal, the farmer said, "Soon as I smoke this pipe, I'll go down an' help right that load o' hay. By the way, where is yore paw?"

The lad answered, "Paw's under the hay."

    ☆   ☆   ☆   ☆   ☆   ☆   ☆

JERRY was the most promising youth in the little town and everyone was confident of his success in life. He announced one day that he was leaving to study law. Six weeks later he returned, and the storekeeper asked:

"Well, Jerry, how's the law?"

He replied, "The law ain't what it's cracked up to be; I'm sorry I learnt it!"

    ☆   ☆   ☆   ☆   ☆   ☆   ☆

ZEKE'S MOTHER had died when he was only a baby and the boy had known nothing but kicks and cuffs from his drunken, shiftless father. One day, Zeke looked out the window of the cabin and saw his father in a life-and-death struggle with a bear. The boy yelled, "Sic 'im, paw; sic 'im bear!"

JEREMIAH was given out to be the laziest man in the county. This particular morning, he and his wife sat on the front porch of their log cabin, his chair tilted with the back resting against the porch railing, her chair facing him as she shelled peas.

"Here comes 'Squire Witherspoon's funeral now," she remarked. "They got the automobile hearse from Marshall and the widow and the two boys is in a fine car. And there are three, four, five other automobiles. And there must be fifteen buggies and wagons behind them.

"I reckon it's the finest funeral procession in the history of our community."

Jeremiah sighed, "Too bad my chair ain't facin' the road so I could see it."

☆   ☆   ☆   ☆   ☆   ☆   ☆

A NATIVE was trudging along the sandy road and not far behind him a dog was trotting. Suddenly a car appeared over the rise; there was the sound of brakes as the driver frantically tried to stop, but the machine struck the dog, killing him instantly.

The motorist sprang out and said, "I'm terribly sorry. I have a dog and I wouldn't have anything happen to him for worlds. I know how you feel."

As the native started to speak, the stranger said. "And I guess you've got a boy at home and he will be broken-hearted. Here's ten dollars; maybe you can get another one to take this poor dog's place."

The motorist climbed back in the car and drove away. The man looked down at the unfortunate animal and at last spoke: "I wonder whose dog he was."

☆   ☆   ☆   ☆   ☆   ☆   ☆

A CHINESE LAUNDRYMAN, out for a stroll through the tall pines near the frontier town, happened to look back and, about twenty paces behind him, was a big bear, sniffing at his footprints. The Chinaman exclaimed, "You like-e my tracks; me make-e you some more!"

☆   ☆   ☆   ☆   ☆   ☆   ☆

HANK'S WIFE was always nagging at him. One day, as Hank stood on the street in the frontier community, a boy ran up and gasped out, "A wildcat has gone in the cabin where your wife is." Hank just stood there.

"Ain't you gonna do nothin' about it?" the lad asked.

"Naw, sir," Hank replied. "That wildcat went in there of his own free will an' accord, an' he'll just have to look out for hisself."

A VALUABLE HORSE had been lost, so the owner had the village editor "strike off" some handbills offering a reward of $10 to the finder. It was the middle of summer and things were quiet, so just about everybody in town — the teacher, the preacher, the doctor, the lawyer, even the editor — turned out to seek the horse.

It wasn't long until the village idiot came into town, leading the animal.

The citizens flocked around and asked, "How did you do it?"

"Oh, it was simple," the half-wit explained. "I just sat down and figgered where I would go if I was a horse, and I went there and there he was!"

☆   ☆   ☆   ☆   ☆   ☆   ☆

A GROUP of farmers was listening to the radio in the crossroads store. The program of fiddle music ended and an orchestra came on, playing "When the Moon Comes Over the Mountain." One of the listeners said, "Turn it off; I never did care for grand opery."

☆   ☆   ☆   ☆   ☆   ☆   ☆

THE traveling salesman, jogging along over a country road in the "piney woods," overtook a long, tall, loose-jointed native and called out, "Want to ride?"

"Don't mind ef I do," the native replied and clambered in. As they rode along, he explained:

"I was in town yistiddy an' they tole me that Joe Smithers was in the day before, and had called me an ornery, egg-suckin', yellow hound, so I'm on my way now to have it out with him."

After a little while, they came in sight of a cabin. Sitting in the front doorway was an individual who was industriously doing nothing. He appeared even longer, taller and looser-jointed than the passenger. The latter said to the driver, "This here's the place."

So the native alighted and approached the other. The traveling man sat in the car to view the rough-and-tumble fight that seemed imminent. The two natives exchanged some words but the distance was such that the "drummer" could not hear what was said.

In a minute or two, however, his acquaintance turned around and walked back to the car, climbed in and, as the drive was resumed, the traveling man eagerly inquired, "What happened?"

"Oh," the other said, "I asked Joe ef he had called me an ornery, egg-suckin', yellow hound and he owned up like a man that he had. Ef he had denied it, I'd a beat him half to death!"

Critters
and
Climate

A POT OF COFFEE was boiling on a camp fire when a norther struck, causing a skim of ice to form on top of the coffee, and this ice had to be broken before the hot coffee could be poured.

☆　☆　☆　☆　☆　☆　☆

THE year of the "big wind" — old-timers say it was in the late '80's — the wind was so strong that it slowed the sun down and finally brought it to a complete halt. So great were the efforts of the sun to resume its course that it grew quite pale, but remained there in one spot so long that at last the stars came out and the sun really was a queer sight, with nine stars clustering around it.

After nearly four hours, the wind wore itself out and the sun was able to go down.

IT GOT so hot one summer in Southeast Texas that the old stumps crawled over and got in the shade.

☆   ☆   ☆   ☆   ☆   ☆   ☆

AND as for wind, it has been known to turn a prairie-dog hole inside out, blow the feathers off of chickens and carry a dozen farm-houses away without disturbing the mortgages on the houses.

☆   ☆   ☆   ☆   ☆   ☆   ☆.

AMARILLO is reputed to have nothing between the city and the North Pole except a barbed wire fence — and one winter it got so cold that Admiral Byrd hurriedly left town to keep from catching double pneumonia.

☆   ☆   ☆   ☆   ☆   ☆   ☆

THAT was the day that the Amarillo zoo's foremost attraction, a polar bear, froze to death.

☆   ☆   ☆   ☆   ☆   ☆   ☆

MOURNFUL MATT decided to have a garden so he planted a few cucumber seed; then — the unaccustomed exertion making him weary — he lay down for a little nap.

When he awoke, he found himself imprisoned in a tangle of vines that had sprung up in just those few minutes. Fortunately, he had one hand free, and so was able to reach his pocket knife, opened it with his teeth and hacked himself loose.

Then he fled down the road, pursued by the vines, for nearly three-quarters of a mile.

Safe at last, he was describing his narrow escape to a friend, who interrupted to ask:

"What's that yellow object sticking out of your pants pocket?"

Matt looked down and pulled out a big cucumber that had ripened and then gone to seed!

☆   ☆   ☆   ☆   ☆   ☆   ☆

THE great Staked Plains stretched out interminably, not a sign of life, day after day, to break the tremendous monotony of cactus, sand and dwarfed mesquite. Then, one morning, on the eastern horizon appeared a tiny speck, and a similar speck appeared on the western horizon.

All day the two specks plodded toward each other, the only moving objects in all that dreary landscape. As they drew closer and closer, it could be discerned that they were men. At last, near the close of the day, when they were only 50 yards apart, one called, "Hey, you!"

The other looked around and then said, "Do you mean me?"

THE little city of Rising Star was struck by a flood a good many years ago as the result of an eight-inch downpour. Next morning, a newspaperman, on the way from Eastland, the county seat, to get the details, encountered the county commissioner of the precinct and said:

"Commissioner, I hear that a full-grown cow was drowned on the main street."

"That's a lie," the official heatedly said; "it was only a two-year-old bull."

☆   ☆   ☆   ☆   ☆   ☆   ☆

PURSUED by a huge timber wolf, a traveler who was on foot back in the early days climbed a big tree and felt safe. The wolf disappeared, but in a little while came back with a small creature dangling from its jaws. It was a beaver, which he had brought to cut down the tree!

☆   ☆   ☆   ☆   ☆   ☆   ☆

"IN THE early days, I was out on the great treeless plains, afoot, as my horse had gotten away during the night," related Cactus Henry. "I looked up and there was a big buffalo bull charging at me.

"So I climbed a tree and——"

A visitor from the East spoke up, "Hold on! I thought you said the plains were treeless."

"That's right," said the old-timer, "but just then I saw one of those wonderful mirages that they have out there. Usually, these mirages appear to be lakes, but sometimes they are houses or other things; this mirage happened to be a forest, so I just shinnied up one of those mirage trees and reached safety.

"Besides, that was a mirage buffalo."

☆   ☆   ☆   ☆   ☆   ☆   ☆

PIZEN JOE got lonesome out on the range and so he made friends with a bullsnake. In fact, they became inseparable pals, and so when the cowboy decided to take a trip on the train to El Paso, he took his snake along, intending to exhibit him there.

Joe was up in the smoking car playing poker when the snake, lonesome for his companionship, got out of the box and started for the coach ahead. The train was half way up a mountain and, just as the creature reached the vestibule, the rear coach came unhooked. The snake realized that if something wasn't done, the car would go rolling back down the mountain, and so he coiled his tail about the hand-brake on one coach and his neck about the hand-brake on the other coach and held them together until the conductor discovered what had happened.

The only thing, the pull had been so great that the bullsnake was stretched to nine times his original length — so Pizen Joe exhibited him as a boa constrictor.

ONE SETTLER worked out a way to cope with the wind: he anchored his house down with log chains. He got the idea from his earlier experience as a captain of a ship.

However, he did not use the anchors and chains except in case of a severe blow as he liked the moderate rocking of the house in an average wind, as the motion reminded him of his days at sea.

☆   ☆   ☆   ☆   ☆   ☆   ☆

THIS SETTLER also set out a rain barrel. Not that it ever had rained, but he wanted to be prepared in case it ever did.

One day, a mighty wind came along and blew the barrel away, carrying it for miles and miles. After a few hours, the wind reversed itself and blew the barrel back to the very spot where it had stood, right under the eaves.

However, the frictional force of the wind, combined with the wear and tear of brush and rocks that the barrel had encountered on its tour, resulted in its having wasted away to a mere keg.

☆   ☆   ☆   ☆   ☆   ☆   ☆

ONE MORNING, a wind came up and blew and blew — it blew so hard that it blew away a barrel that was sitting in a yard; well, not to mislead you, it didn't blow the entire barrel away — it left the bunghole.

The rancher took the bunghole to town the next Saturday and had the coopersmith build a new barrel around it.

You learn to conserve things in West Texas.

☆   ☆   ☆   ☆   ☆   ☆   ☆

AN EASTERNER was driving along a heavy stretch of sand, and he stopped to let the steaming motor cool. He asked a man on horseback, "How far does this sand extend?"

The native said, "About a mile."

"But," the tourist protested, "I've already come further than that!"

"Oh, I mean straight down," explained the horseman.

☆   ☆   ☆   ☆   ☆   ☆   ☆

THEY don't have many rivers in West Texas but there is a tale about one stream, in an almost inaccessible region, where the water is warm, the reason being that it flows over rocks with such rapidity that the friction heats it.

If the tourist doesn't register disbelief, his informant is liable to tell him about a recent trip down this river when the water grew hotter and hotter — so much so that the bottom of the boat actually made blisters on his feet through his cowboy boots. Then he will conclude:

"And I caught a big fish that was follerin' the boat, and when I pulled him in, he was cooked to a turn!"

"WHAT's the most buffalo you ever saw at one time?" a school-marm who was vacationing in Texas asked a grizzled frontiers-man.

"About 4,000,000, I reckon," he drawled.

"Four million!" she exclaimed.

"Yep, maybe a few more; it was back in 1879 an' one mornin' before we had broke camp, we saw 'em a-comin' an' it was all we fourteen men could do to kill 'em fast enough to keep 'em from tramplin' us to death. Our gun-barrels wuz red-hot an' we kept up the slaughter more than twenty-four hours.

"Finally, the last ones had passed by, and we broke camp an' crossed the Colorado an' reached the hills — an' it was none too soon, neither."

"Why?" asked the visitor.

"Because here come the main herd."

☆ ☆ ☆ ☆ ☆ ☆ ☆

CROSS a scrub cow with a locomotive and you'll get a full-blood Jersey every time.

☆ ☆ ☆ ☆ ☆ ☆ ☆

WHEN told that eggs were 60 cents a dozen, the "town grouch" at Denton growled, "Why, that's a nickle a-piece."

"Yes," the grocer reminded him, "but an egg is a day's work for a hen."

☆ ☆ ☆ ☆ ☆ ☆ ☆

Two OLD-TIMERS in East Texas were telling about their fishing exploits down at the village store while a big crowd listened to the verbal contest.

At last Uncle Jake yelled: "Listen, you snaggle-toothed old toad! Once I caught a 50-pound bass with just a rusty old pin."

But Dad came right back: "About two year ago I pulled up an old lantern dated 1861 while fishing near Aransas Pass, and, believe it or not, that lantern was still burning."

Uncle Jake said: "Looky here, Dad, there's no use lyin' about it; I'll take 45 pounds off my fish if you'll just blow out that dog-gone lantern."

☆ ☆ ☆ ☆ ☆ ☆ ☆

"THE biggest rattler I ever saw?" mused Rawhide Henry, in answer to a question from a tourist.

"Well, I killed one onct on Palo Pinto Creek that was 32 feet long — that is, the snake, not the creek.

"Yes, sir, that snake measured sixteen feet from the tip of his nose to the tip of his tail, and sixteen feet from the tip of his tail to the tip of his nose — thirty-two feet in all."

AND then there was the snake that got hold of some moonshine whiskey and got delirium tremens and saw purple men.

☆ ☆ ☆ ☆ ☆ ☆ ☆

"DAYLIGHT SLIM" was given out to be the most accomplished liar in West Texas, so when he rode into town one day, the boys in the saloon clamored, "Tell us a lie, Slim."

"No, boys," he responded, "I'm through tellin' 'em. An' you know what cured me? It was that elk that I been claimin' all these years that I killed — you remember, the elk with the seventeen-foot horn-spread and I ust to tell you that I kept the horns up in the loft at my shack.

"Well, I told that lie so many times that I got to believin' it myself, an' a few nights ago, I actually lit the lantern an' climbed up in the loft to see them horns.

"And durned ef they wasn't there!

"So, boys, I'm through tellin' lies."

☆ ☆ ☆ ☆ ☆ ☆ ☆

MAJOR TOM KING, former State Auditor, tells this one:

Two mosquitoes grabbed a man off his horse as he was riding along a road near the Gulf Coast, and one said:

"Let's carry him into the swamp."

The other objected:

"No, let's eat him here — if we carry him into the swamp, the big mosquitoes will take him away from us."

☆ ☆ ☆ ☆ ☆ ☆ ☆

ON ONE occasion, Major King was investigating the rather involved financial affairs of an oil town that had slumped rather badly after the boom was over. A bond issue had been sold when there seemed little in the way of solid assets to base it on. He kept pressing the man who had handled the deal but received only evasive answers.

The financier knew that King was intensely proud of the history of Texas and of his native state, Tennessee, so at last when a direct answer had to be made, the man said:

"I want to tell you, sir, that not one dollar of those bonds was sold south of the Mason and Dixon line!"

☆ ☆ ☆ ☆ ☆ ☆ ☆

GIB MORGAN, the Paul Bunyan of the oil fields, dug the ditch for the first pipe-line. He used a drove of razorbacks that he trained to root in a straight line.

☆ ☆ ☆ ☆ ☆ ☆ ☆

A RAZORBACK is, of course, the thinnest possible piece of pork connecting a snout and a tail.

"I NEVER expected no trouble that morning when I was out on a little stroll," Brazos Jim related, "when, suddenly, there came a mountain lion straight at me, his jaws wide open.

"There was only one thing to do an' I done it; I stuck my arm down his throat about two feet, grabbed a hold an' give a big pull an' turned him wrong-side out!

"O' course, this had him facing in the opposite direction an' he ran off.

"Then I resumed my stroll."

    ☆   ☆   ☆   ☆   ☆   ☆   ☆

THE razorback derives his name from his habit of stropping himself against a stump.

    ☆   ☆   ☆   ☆   ☆   ☆   ☆

"WE FOUND a little pig wanderin' in the woods and brought it home an' tuck care of it for a good while," young Eddie was relating to his cousin, who lived in town.

"Then what happened?"

"The neighbor who owned the critter came over an' claimed it."

"So you had to give it up; that was too bad," the town boy sympathized.

"Well," the rural cousin said, "we did have the use of the pig for three months."

    ☆   ☆   ☆   ☆   ☆   ☆   ☆

"As A hog roots for his food, he throws his weight on the right hind leg," read a sign in a Fort Worth cafe. "All our hams come from the left side only—they're the tenderest."

    ☆   ☆   ☆   ☆   ☆   ☆   ☆

UP IN Cooke County, the soil is so rich that a farmer drops a kernel of corn in the ground and then jumps to one side.

The corn stalks grow so big that plans are being made to sell them for use as telephone poles.

    ☆   ☆   ☆   ☆   ☆   ☆   ☆

ON ONE especially rich piece of ground, a boy climbed a corn-stalk to see out over the surrounding country, and the stalk grew so fast that he was unable to climb down. Soon, he was out of sight.

His father and the hired man grabbed axes to save him from death by starvation, but the stalk grew so swiftly that the axes couldn't hit twice in the same place.

The boy lived on green corn for a week and threw down three bushels of cobs. By this time, he had reached the frigid stratosphere but was rescued, barely in time, by a very daring aviator — from Texas, of course.

A TEXAS hen laid a square egg and cackled, "Ouch."

☆　☆　☆　☆　☆　☆　☆

FOR YEARS, fishermen had tried to land a catfish that was known as "the Big Un." At last, one summer, men and boys gathered in great numbers and, after much excitement, hauled the fish ashore, age, no doubt, having reduced his power to resist.

The flesh was salted down and the whole countryside feasted on it for almost two years.

You can get some idea of Big Un's size from the fact that most of his scales were used as shingles and those not used in this way were fitted with handles and made excellent shovels — a few of which are still in use in Cass County.

☆　☆　☆　☆　☆　☆　☆

"TEX" EASLEY, Washington correspondent, declares: "I kept a giant Rio Grande Valley pink grapefruit displayed on my fireplace and still some of my neighbors wouldn't believe it.

"Finally, during a severe shortage last Winter, one of the hospitals here requisitioned the grapefruit to keep up the citrus diet for their patients a couple of weeks."

That must have been one of the smaller ones that somebody palmed off on Easley.

☆　☆　☆　☆　☆　☆　☆

A WATERMELON grower in Parker County, famed for its huge and luscious melons, is working on an idea: a watermelon that will whistle when it is ripe, thus eliminating the risk of cutting a melon that isn't ready to be eaten.

The method, which is said to have advanced beyond the experimental stage, consists of inserting a plug with a whistle attachment when the melon is small; as it ripens, gas forms, blowing the whistle, and informing the grower that it is ready to harvest.

A field of melons, so equipped, will sound a good deal like a convention of football referees, whistles all tooting at once.

It is possible that the system can be improved so that the whistles will play simple tunes, which will entertain the pickers.

☆　☆　☆　☆　☆　☆　☆

CROPS in one section were so bad one season on account of the drouth that the crows had to lie on their stomach to eat the corn.

☆　☆　☆　☆　☆　☆　☆

CONVERSING with an Easterner who had stopped for gasoline and oil, the filling station proprietor swung an arm in the general direction of the sandy wilderness and said, "All we need is some good people and water."

"Yes," said the tourist as he stepped on the starter, "and that's all h—— needs, too!"

AN OLD-TIMER swears that, in his youth, he lassoed a big steer on the banks of the Llano River and, just as he made the catch, the animal jerked the slack out of the rope, and the rope flipped his expensive watch out of his pocket into a deep hole of water that was known as the home of big fish.

About four years later, he returned to the same spot to fish. Presently he snagged a big bass that weighed at least 10 pounds. The fish had a large knot on its jaw, and our hero was just about to throw it back when he decided to investigate the fish's swelling. Of course, the knot on the fish's jaw was caused by the presence of that high-priced watch. Moreover, the watch's stem had become entangled in the fish's gills so that it was wound every time the fish breathed. It had lost only 10 seconds in four years.

☆ ☆ ☆ ☆ ☆ ☆ ☆

A TOURIST, commenting on the extreme heat in the great open spaces, was informed by a citizen:

"This ain't hot. You shoulda been here three years ago. Why, it was so hot that summer that the trees just naturally melted down and run off."

And to prove his statement, he waved his hand around and said, "You see all the trees are gone."

☆ ☆ ☆ ☆ ☆ ☆ ☆

THE farmer had bought a new hoe-handle which he tossed on the ground, not noticing that a rattlesnake was nearby. The angry reptile struck the handle, which began swelling and swelling until it was a huge log.

So the farmer took the log to the mill and had it made into lumber. There was sufficient for a house, not a big house, just four rooms with a hall down the middle and a front porch and a back porch. Then there was enough material left for a neat fence.

The farmer had one all the construction himself and, now that the house was completed, he was in the front room gazing around with pride at his work, when he was horror-stricken — the walls were closing in on him; the effect of the venom was dying out!

He escaped to the outside barely in time to keep from being choked to death.

The material continued to shrivel until it reached its normal size, the house becoming no bigger than a cigar box, which was surrounded by a line of tooth-picks!

☆ ☆ ☆ ☆ ☆ ☆ ☆

IT GETS so dry in some parts of West Texas that the citizens fasten stamps on letters with safety-pins.

"My Fellow Country-men"

THE orator at a political picnic declaimed, "As we swing about over mighty Texas, from the piney woods on the east to the boundless plains of the Panhandle, and on to the deep recesses of the Big Bend canyon——"

A matter-of-fact voice broke in, "Let me off at Uvalde; that's where I live."

☆   ☆   ☆   ☆   ☆   ☆   ☆

UNITED STATES MARSHAL GUY MCNAMARA of Waco tells of an old-time race in which a candidate accused his opponent of inconsistency and likened him to "the big snake that went through the county":

"He wobbled in and he wobbled out;
He kept the people all in doubt
As to whether the snake that made the track
Was coming in or going back."

A TEXAS NEWSPAPER on the morning of the 1944 national election predicted the weather:

"Not Dewey."

☆   ☆   ☆   ☆   ☆   ☆   ☆

AND on the eve of the meeting of the University of Texas regents at which the university president was ousted, the forecast was:

"Not Rainey."

☆   ☆   ☆   ☆   ☆   ☆   ☆

THE justice of the peace had been in office a long time and was past 60 years of age. His young opponent, a college graduate, went around and murmured in the voters' ears, "Did you know that my opponent is a sexagenarian?", emphasizing the first syllable in a sinister way — and the shocked voters elected the young fellow overwhelmingly.

☆   ☆   ☆   ☆   ☆   ☆   ☆

IF THE cost of government keeps rising, they'll have to change the spelling of the State's name to T-A-X-E-S.

☆   ☆   ☆   ☆   ☆   ☆   ☆

TWO ACQUAINTANCES met in the hotel lobby in Austin during a session of the legislature, and one greeted the other with:

"How are you doing — and who?"

☆   ☆   ☆   ☆   ☆   ☆   ☆

THE candidate was attending a country picnic, and he moved around through the crowd, shaking hands. Many of the faces were unfamiliar to him, but he greeted each man as though they were old-time friends. To one young farmer, he said, "Mighty glad to see you — and how is your father?"

The voter said, "Paw died four years ago."

"Of course, of course," the candidate said, hastily, "I recall that very well."

As he continued through the shifting crowd, he met this same farmer but did not recognize him and, after another hearty handshake, he inquired, "And how is your father?"

The farmer replied, "Paw is still dead."

☆   ☆   ☆   ☆   ☆   ☆   ☆

THE Republican candidate for Congress in the Dallas district was proclaiming the grandeur of the G.O.P. when a listener called out, "Hurray for the Democratic Party!"

"Why are you a Democrat?" the candidate demanded.

"Well," the citizen hesitated, "well, my father was a Democrat."

"And suppose," the speaker asked, "your father had been a horse-thief?"

"Well, in that case, I'd be a Republican," was the answer.

THE Fourth-of-July orator shouted, "I know no North; I know no South; I know no East; I know no West!"

A boy yelled, "Mister, you better brush up on your geography."

☆   ☆   ☆   ☆   ☆   ☆   ☆

HARLEY SADLER, the famed tent-show owner-comedian who is also a member of the legislature, was asked by a House member:

"What did you think about my speech?"

Tactfully, Sadler replied, "It was all right but it could have been three minutes shorter."

"But," the other said, "I only spoke three minutes."

"I know," Sadler replied as he walked away.

☆   ☆   ☆   ☆   ☆   ☆   ☆

THE speaker at a political rally in Beaumont was a leading lawyer, but his voice was better adapted to a courtroom than to the great outdoors and a listener on the edge of the crowd broke in with, "Louder! Louder!"

After he had been thus interrupted three times, the speaker said:

"My friends, on that last day, when Gabriel shall stand on the loftiest mountain peak and lift up his golden trumpet and sound the notes that proclaim that time shall be no more, I have no doubt that some durn fool from Beaumont will yell, 'Louder, Gabe, louder!'"

☆   ☆   ☆   ☆   ☆   ☆   ☆

THEY were going to hold a special election to fill the office of sheriff, vacated by death. It being an election and not a party primary, negroes could vote and one of the candidates, whose reputation was not too savory, said:

"Uncle Henry, I hope you'll vote for me."

The old darkey whom he was addressing replied:

"Well, suh, you is my second choice."

Thinking that he could eliminate the negro's first choice by a little plain and fancy smearing, the aspirant inquired:

"And who is your first choice?"

Uncle Henry replied, "Jes' anybody, suh, jes' anybody."

☆   ☆   ☆   ☆   ☆   ☆   ☆

A FARMER drove up Congress Avenue in Austin in a buggy and, stopping in front of a store, he said to a man on the sidewalk, "Mister, will you hold my horse for a few minutes?"

The other drew himself up and replied, "Sir, I am a State Senator!"

"Thanks for tellin' me," the farmer said, "but I'll trust you."

THE candidate declaimed, "Fellow citizens, I have helped kill off the buffalo and bring in the cattle; I fought Indians; I captured bad men——"

A citizen broke in, "You've done enough for your country; go home and rest; I'm going to vote for the other fellow."

☆ ☆ ☆ ☆ ☆ ☆ ☆

FORMER District Attorney Fred Erisman of Longview made a race for Attorney General but finished third. Next day, he received a wire from a friend, "Never mind; Lincoln was defeated, too." Erisman remarked, "And I didn't even know Lincoln was running."

☆ ☆ ☆ ☆ ☆ ☆ ☆

THERE are a good many citizens of Swedish ancestry in Texas, and back in 1932 when it appeared that the governor's race was going to be close (and it was), a political scout went out to try and find out what the sentiment was among that element.

"Mr. Jensen, who is going to win — Mrs. Ferguson or Ross Sterling?"

"I yust wouldn't want to say," was the cautious reply.

"Well, who do you think has the best show?"

His features lighted up, "Oh, Ringling Bros., they bane have the best show."

☆ ☆ ☆ ☆ ☆ ☆ ☆

THE member of the House from Jasper County arose at his desk and said:

"Mr. Speaker and fellow members: If you raise corn, it's yores, ain't it? And if you grind that corn into meal and make it into cornbread and eat it, it's yores, ain't it?

"And if you make hominy out of that corn, it's yores, ain't it?

"Then if you take corn and make a gallon of whiskey out of it to drink, why in the name of justice ain't it yores?"

☆ ☆ ☆ ☆ ☆ ☆ ☆

ONE GOVERNOR was noted — or notorious — for his free (?) use of the pardoning power. It is said that when a relative of a convict visited him to plead for clemency, the governor would point out the window and remark, "There's a mighty nice bull, out there; how much will you give me for him?" The bull was sold eighty-seven times — and was still grazing in the governor's corral when the administration ended.

☆ ☆ ☆ ☆ ☆ ☆ ☆

WHEN James V. Allred was making his first race for governor, he touched up a rival: "I was listening to the radio the other night and I heard my opponent giving me thunder for using the radio — and he was talking over the radio himself at the time."

AND in this same race, Allred said that his competitor claimed to be for a "blended tax." Allred threw this challenge:

"What is a blended tax?"

"I have heard of blended coffee and I have heard of blended whiskey — and old-timers say there was more blend than there was whiskey.

"I looked it up in the dictionary and here is what I found: Blend — To mix or mingle so that which is mixed or mingled can not be distinguished or individually separated."

☆   ☆   ☆   ☆   ☆   ☆   ☆

THE new member of the city council was a self-made man, and he had been elected on an economy platform. At his first meeting, the city's new park was discussed and one member said:

"I move that we buy six gondolas to put on the lake."

The new councilman spoke up, "I move that we buy a pair of gondolas and let nature take its course."

☆   ☆   ☆   ☆   ☆   ☆   ☆

PROBABLY oldest of all the political stories:

A high-type citizen was induced to make his first race for office.

The campaign took on momentum and the opposing candidate made a sharp attack on his rival in a speech. That individual next morning was mourning to his campaign manager:

"Why, in two weeks, he'll be accusing me of stealing a horse!"

His manager rejoined:

"Accuse, nothing! He'll prove it on you."

☆   ☆   ☆   ☆   ☆   ☆   ☆

A MAN was elected governor on the promise to put the penitentiary on a paying basis — but he forgot to say on a paying basis to whom.

☆   ☆   ☆   ☆   ☆   ☆   ☆

THE Capitol of Texas is the largest state capitol in the United States; in fact, it is even higher than the national capitol. A philosophic politician, who had long observed the activities of lobbyists, was strolling down the broad avenue with a friend. He looked back at the mighty dome and asked, "Bill, do you know why the Capitol is still there?"

"Why?" the other asked.

"Because it's just too big to carry off."

☆   ☆   ☆   ☆   ☆   ☆   ☆

A MAN who hit it rich from the discovery of oil decided to enter politics. At the end of one term, his fortune was gone, and a political foe said, "I can sum up his career in six words: **Rich by accident, poor by ignorance.**"

"AND NOW," said the long-winded speaker, "I must tax your patience."

"Good heavens," muttered a listener, "are they going to tax that, too?"

☆   ☆   ☆   ☆   ☆   ☆   ☆

OF A certain State politician, a man remarked, "Brown is a man of few words — but he uses them often."

☆   ☆   ☆   ☆   ☆   ☆   ☆

"LOUDER!" shouted a listener in the rear of the hall after a speaker with a weak voice had been talking a few minutes.

A man on the front row raised up, turned around, and asked, "Can't you hear?"

"Not a word."

"Well," the man up front said, "you ain't missed a durn thing."

☆   ☆   ☆   ☆   ☆   ☆   ☆

SIMILAR is the one about the lecturer who was a guest in a farmhome before speaking at the rural school that night. At supper, he ate almost nothing, explaining, "Before I make a speech, I never eat." The old lady could not attend the meeting on account of her rheumatism, so afterward she asked her husband, "How was the speech?"

The farmer replied, "He might as well have et."

☆   ☆   ☆   ☆   ☆   ☆   ☆

AND still similar is the one about the noted man who made an address in a small town and next morning met an elderly woman on the street. She said, "We had company and I didn't get to hear your speech."

He replied with an air of assumed modesty, "Oh, you didn't miss much."

"Yes," she replied, "that's what everybody is saying this morning."

☆   ☆   ☆   ☆   ☆   ☆   ☆

THE candidate for State office was getting ready to open his campaign.

"Only thing I'm afraid of is they'll find out that my father was hanged," he confided to friends.

"The press agent will fix that up all right," they reassured him — and the publicity man wrote:

"During a public spectacle, the candidate's father fell from a scaffolding and death was instantaneous."

☆   ☆   ☆   ☆   ☆   ☆   ☆

A MAN was being tried for murder. One of the attorneys for the defendant had resigned not long before from the State Highway Commission after there had been great clamor through the newspapers.

The star witness for the State in the murder trial had been brought back from Huntsville, where he was serving a term for seventeen felonies to which he had pleaded guilty. On cross examination, one of the defense lawyers asked:

"You stole a bale of cotton at Midlothian, didn't you?"

"Yes."

"You stole an automobile from Ranger, didn't you?"

"Yes."

"You broke into the depot at Mangum and robbed it, didn't you?"

"I didn't break in; the door was unlocked; but I did rob it."

And then the witness flared up, "I done all them things and fourteen other felonies, besides — but I ain't never done time on the State Highway Commission like yore pardner has."

☆   ☆   ☆   ☆   ☆   ☆   ☆

A MEMBER of the House was making a speech in favor of Gov. W. Lee O'Daniel's proposed "transaction tax" which would have levied a tax on practically every business transaction. However, the first sale of crops was exempt.

Another legislator broke in, "The bill would hit livestock raisers — those who raise horses and mules."

The proponent said, "No, horses are plainly exempt; the bill says horticulture."

☆   ☆   ☆   ☆   ☆   ☆   ☆

THE sheriff had not been exactly a shining success in administering the office, but he decided to ask a second term and started handing out cards. A citizen took one and remarked, "You are in office now, aren't you?" The sheriff said, "Yes," and the voter declared, "I'll be glad to help you out."

☆   ☆   ☆   ☆   ☆   ★   ☆

ABOUT as telling a retort as could be made to a heckler was that of Congressman Jack Beal, who was making a speech for the renowned Joseph Weldon Bailey. Someone yelled, "Bailey is beaten!" Beal said, "My friend, you may be right; but let me remind you that grand old Sam Houston was once a candidate for Governor and was beaten, but only an expert librarian today can tell you the name of the man who defeated him."

☆   ☆   ☆   ☆   ☆   ☆   ☆

A CANDIDATE at a barbecue declaimed:

"Texas is the brightest star on the American flag and I'm for her, right or wrong. That's my platform, and if my opponent doesn't like it, let him go back to where I came from."

TALKING about a clique with which he disagreed, Fisher Alsup, noted raconteur said, "None of them is staggering around under a store of knowledge sufficient to give them flat feet."

☆   ☆   ☆   ☆   ☆   ☆   ☆

"I CAN'T remember a more effective political speech than was made in Killeen in a race for justice of the peace," narrated Alsup. He went on:

"The incumbent was asking a second term, and he was a good speaker and was very popular. His opponent wore thick glasses, a claw-hammer coat and a derby hat, and had a piping voice.

"Well, after the 'squire had made an appeal for a second term, the other man climbed up on the platform and peered around for half a minute at the crowd through those glasses, and then he said:

'My opponent complains because he ain't had the office but one term. Shucks! I ain't had it nary'n yit!'

"The crowd shrieked with glee, pulled him down, carried him around on their shoulders and he was elected."

Alsup drolly concluded, "He was like Balaam's ass — one speech made him famous."

☆   ☆   ☆   ☆   ☆   ☆   ☆

THE statesman spoke on and on. Just outside the door, a man asked a friend who was leaving, "Has he finished?" The other replied, "Yes, a long time ago, but he won't quit."

One listener pulled out his watch, looked at it, then held it to his ear to see if it was still running.

Finally, a man on the front row went to sleep and began snoring. The speaker exclaimed to a small boy sitting beside the sleeping one, "Wake him up." The lad replied, "Wake him up yourself; you put him to sleep."

EVERY TIME Jenkins visited Houston, he went to his favorite seafood cafe and ordered his favorite delicacy — broiled lobster. But, every time, he was served with a lobster that had a claw missing. At last he complained to the waiter. Pierre shrugged his shoulders and explained:

"M'sieur, it ees lak thees; the lobsters zey are in a beeg basket and zey geet to fighting and one tears zee claw off of anuzzer."

"Well," said the visitor, "next time, bring me a winner."

Coming Off the Trail

THERE have been tales told by the men who went up the trail with herds of Longhorns in the long ago, but Jack Potter, son of the Rev. Jack Potter, famed as "the fighting parson," tells of his experiences on the return trip, which he made by train:

Now, reader, here I was, a boy not yet seventeen years old, 2,000 miles from home. I had never been on a railroad train, had never slept in a hotel, never taken a bath in a bathhouse and, from babyhood, I had heard terrible stories about ticket thieves, money-changers, pickpockets, three-card monte and other robbing schemes, and I had horrors about this my first railroad trip.

The first thing I did was to make my money safe by tying it up in my shirt-tail; I had a draft for $150 and some currency. I purchased a second-hand trunk and about two hundred feet of rope with which to tie it. The contents of the trunk were one apple-horn saddle, a pair of chaps, a Colt's .45, one sugan, a hen-skin blanket and a change of dirty clothes.

The company had agreed to provide me with transportation and they purchased a local ticket to Denver and gave me a letter to deliver to the general ticket agent at this point, instructing him to sell me a reduced ticket to Dodge City, Kansas, and enable me to secure a cowboy ticket from there to San Antonio for twenty-five dollars.

About 4 p. m. the Union Pacific train came pulling into Greeley. Then it was a hasty handshake with the boys — one of them handed me my trunk check, saying, "Your baggage is loaded" — and the train pulled out. It took several minutes for me to collect myself and then the conductor came through and called for tickets. When I handed him my ticket, he punched a hole in it and then pulled out a red slip, punched it too and slipped it into my hatband. I jumped to my feet and said, "You can't come that on me; give me back my ticket." But he passed out of hearing and, as I had not yet learned how to walk on a moving train, I could not follow him.

When I had become fairly settled in my seat again, the train crossed a bridge and, as it went by, I thought the thing was going to hit me on the head. I dodged those bridges all the way up to Denver.

When I reached there, I got off at the Union Station and walked down to the baggage car and saw them unloading my trunk. I stepped up and said, "I will take my trunk." A man said, "No, we are handling this baggage." "But," said I, "that is my trunk and has my saddle and gun in it." They paid no attention to me and wheeled the trunk off to the baggage room but I followed right along, determined that they were not going to put anything over me.

Seeing that I was so insistent, one of the men asked me for my check. It was wrapped up in my shirt-tail and I went after it and produced the draft I had been given as wages. He said, "This is not your trunk check; where is your metal check with numbers on it?" Then it began to dawn on me what the darn thing was and when I produced it and handed it to him, he asked me where I was going. I told him San Antonio, Texas, if I could get there. He said, "Now, boy, you leave this trunk right here and we will recheck it and you need not bother about it." That sounded bully to me.

I followed the crowd down Sixteenth and Curtiss Streets and rambled around looking for a quiet place to stop. I found the St. Charles Hotel and made arrangements to stay all night. Then

I went off to a barber shop to get my hair cut and clean up a bit. When the barber finished with me, he asked if I wanted a bath and when I said, "Yes," a negro porter took me down the hallway and into a side room.

He turned on the water, tossed me a couple of towels and disappeared. I commenced undressing hurriedly, fearing the tub would fill up before I could get ready. The water was within a few inches of the top of the tub when I plunged in. Then I gave a yell like a Comanche Indian, for the water was boiling hot! I came out of the tub on all fours but, when I landed on the marble floor, it was so slick that I slipped and fell backwards with my head down. I scrambled promiscuously and finally got my footing with a chair for a brace. I thought: "Jack Potter, you are scalded after the fashion of a hog." I caught a lock of my hair to see if it would "slip," and at the same time fanning myself with my big Stetson hat. I next examined my toe nails for they had received a little more dipping than my hair but I found them in fairly good shape, turning a bit dark but still hanging on.

The next morning, I started out to find the Santa Fe ticket office, where I presented my letter to the head man there. He was a nice-appearing gentleman and, when he had looked over my letter, he said:

"So you are a genuine cowboy? Where is your gun and how many notches have you on its handle? I suppose you carry plenty of salt with you on the trail for emergency? I was just reading in a magazine a few days ago about a large herd which stampeded and one of the punchers mounted a swift horse and ran up in front of the leaders and began throwing out salt, and stopped the herd just in time to keep them from running off a high precipice."

He gave me an emigrant cowboy ticket to Dodge City and a letter to the agent at that place, stating that I was eligible for a cowboy ticket to San Antonio. As it was near train time, I hunted up the baggage crew and told them I was ready to make another start. I showed them my ticket and asked about my trunk. They examined it, put on a new check and gave me one with several numbers on it. I wanted to take my trunk out and put it on the train but they told me to rest easy and they would put it on. I stood right there until I saw them put it on the train, then I climbed aboard.

This being my second day out, I thought my troubles should be over but not so, for I couldn't face those bridges. They kept me dodging and fighting my head. An old gentleman who sat near me said, "Young man, I see by your dress that you are a typical cowboy and, no doubt, you can master the worst bronco or rope and tie a steer in less than a minute; but in riding on a railway train, you seem to be a novice. Sit down on this seat with your back to the front and those bridges won't bother you." And, sure enough, it was just as he said.

We reached Dodge City, where I had to lay over for twenty-four hours. The first acquaintance I met here was George W. Saunders. I also found Jess Presnall and Slim Johnson, as well as several others whom I knew down in Texas. Presnall said, "Jack, you will have lots of company on your way home. Old 'Dog Face' is up here from Cotulla and he and his whole bunch are going back tonight. Old Dog Face is one of the best trail men that ever drove a cow but he is all worked up about having to go back on a train. I wish you would help them along down the line in changing cars."

Dog Face and his bunch were pretty badly frightened and we had considerable difficulty in getting them aboard. It was about 12:30 when the train pulled out. The conductor came around and I gave him my cowboy ticket. It was almost as long as your arm and, as he tore off a chunk of it, I said, "What authority do you have to tear up a man's ticket?" He laughed and said, "You are on my division; I simply tore off one coupon and each conductor between here and San Antonio will tear off one for each division." That sounded all right but I wondered if that ticket would hold out all the way down.

Everyone seemed to be tired and worn out and the bunch began bedding down. Old Dog Face was out of humor and was the last one to bed down. At about 3 o'clock, our train was sidetracked to let the west-bound train pass. This little stop caused the boys to sleep sounder. Just then the west-bound train sped by, traveling at the rate of about forty miles an hour and, just as it passed our coach, the engineer blew the whistle.

Talk about your stampede! That bunch of sleeping cowboys arose as one man and started on the run with old Dog Face in the lead. I was a little slow in getting off but fell in with the drags. I had not yet woke up but, thinking I was in a genuine cattle stampede, yelled out, "Circle your leaders and keep up the drags."

Just then the leaders circled and ran into the drags, knocking some of us down. They circled again and the news butcher crawled out from under foot and jumped through the window like a frog. Before they could circle back the next time, the train crew pushed in the door and caught old Dog Face and soon the bunch quieted down. The conductor was pretty angry and threatened to have us transferred to the freight department and loaded into a stock car.

At Austin, a lively bunch joined us. Pretty soon, the porter called out, "San Antonio, Santonnie-o," and that was music to my ears. My first move in getting off the car was to look for my trunk and found it had arrived. I said to myself, "Jack Potter, you're a lucky dog. Ticket held out all right, toe nails all healed up and trunk came through in good shape."

After registering at the Central Hotel, I wrote to that general ticket agent at Denver:

"I landed in San Antonio this afternoon all O.K. My trunk also came through without a scratch. I want to thank you very much for the man you sent along to look after my trunk. He was very accomodating and would not allow me to assist in loading it at Denver.

"No doubt, he will want to see some of the sights of San Antonio for it is a great place and noted for its chile con carne. When he takes a fill of this food, as every visitor does, you can expect him back in Denver on very short notice as he will be seeking a cooler climate.

"Did you ever eat any chile con carne? I will send you a dozen cans soon but tell your wife to keep it in the refrigerator as it might set the house on fire. Thank you again for past favors.

"Your Bulliest Friend,

JACK POTTER."

A COUPLE of Dallas hunters suddenly discovered that a bull was charging down toward them. They tossed away their guns and raced for safety. One climbed a small tree that barely put him out of reach of the animal's horns and the other man jumped into a hole. He sprang out in a moment and the bull wheeled and rushed toward him, whereupon the man jumped back in the hole, but in a little bit he sprang out again.

His friend up the tree yelled, "Henry, for goodness' sake, stay in there so the bull will go away."

The other said, "There's a wildcat in this hole!"

Justice, More or Less

JUDGE ROY BEAN, the "law west of the Pecos," once was a championship prize fight impresario. Texas authorities had refused to permit the holding of a fight between Bob Fitzsimmons and Peter Maher in the State, so old Roy said, "Bring the fight here," and fighters and fans arrived in Langtry on special trains. Bean sold lots of beer, then escorted the contingent over a pontoon bridge to the Mexico side of the Rio Grande and there the fight was held.

The encounter was brief. Maher came out for the first round, made two or three feints, and then the freckled Fitzsimmons landed one of his famed haymakers and that was all.

A spectator sadly related, "I turned my head to spit and when I looked around, the fight was over."

THE attorney shouted, "Gentlemen of the jury, my client is as pure as the dew-drop that sparkles on the tail of a Texas bull as he rises from his grassy couch and bellows in the face of the rising sun!"

☆　☆　☆　☆　☆　☆　☆

THE young lawyer was arguing his first case. "Gentlemen of the jury," he declaimed, "there are twenty-four hogs involved in this suit — just exactly twice the number in the jury box."

☆　☆　☆　☆　☆　☆　☆

JUDGE ED HILL, the droll jurist who presided over district court in Eastland for years, was trying a case and the first witness, an elderly negress, prefaced each answer with, "I thinks it wuz dis way —."

The judge admonished her, "Aunty, never mind what you think; just answer the questions."

After he had cautioned her for the third time, she said, "Looky heah, Jedge; I ain't no lawyer — I can't talk without thinkin'."

☆　☆　☆　☆　☆　☆　☆

IT IS related that a man was brought to trial in Cotulla years ago on a charge of violating the liquor law. Exhibit "A" consisted of a pint of whiskey. The jury retired, taking the bottle with them. When they filed back into the courtroom, they brought the bottle back — empty.

The foreman announced the verdict, "We the jury find the defendant not guilty, due to insufficient evidence."

☆　☆　☆　☆　☆　☆　☆

A RICH MAN was accused of murder and the evidence at the examining trial was very serious — so serious that not only did friends employ one of the leading lawyers in the State but a nephew slipped around to a prospective juror and said, "Johnson, if you get on that jury and make a successful fight for a verdict of manslaughter, I'll pay you a thousand dollars."

The man agreed and, in due course, was selected on the jury. After the testimony was concluded, the attorney for the defendant made a brilliant speech, which left the courtroom ankle-deep in tears.

For three days and nights, the jury was out but at last came in with a verdict of manslaughter and a term of four years in the penitentiary.

Afterward, the nephew handed the juror the agreed amount and said, "You earned it, all right."

The man said, "You're durn tootin' I did! Why those eleven fools wanted to turn him loose!"

LLOYD GREGORY, managing editor of the Houston Post, tells this one:

A negro was brought into court for trial and the clerk began reading the indictment: "State of Texas vs. Mose Jones."

The defendant moaned, "Good Gawd, what a majority!"

☆　☆　☆　☆　☆　☆　☆

HERE IS a will that a Dutchman in an East Texas county is supposed to have written:

"I am writing of my will mineselluf, that d—— lawyer want he should have too much money, he ask too many answers about family. first thing i want i don't want my brother rudolph get a d—— thing what i got. he is a mumser, he done me out of forty dollars fourteen years since. i want that gretchen my sister she gets the north sixtie akers of at where i am homing it now. i bet she don't get that loafer husban of hers to broke twenty akers next plowing time.

"She can't have it if she lets rudolph liver on it. i want i should have it back if she does. tell momma that six hundred dollars she been looking for for twenty years is berried from the backhouse behind about ten feet down. she better let little otto do the digging and count it when he comes up.

"Momma the rest should get but i want it that hans should tell her what not she shud do so no more slick irishers sell her vokum cleaners. day noise like h—— and a broom don't cost so much. i want it that mine brother heinrich should be my exeter and i want it that the judge should pleeze make plenty bond put up and watch him like h——

"He is good business man but only a dumkopf wood trust him with a busted pfennig. i want d—— sure that rudolph don't get nothing. dat sure fix rudolph."

☆　☆　☆　☆　☆　☆　☆

THE county's richest man was charged with murder and he retained a brilliant young attorney to defend him. Despite the utmost efforts of his counsel, however, the defendant was sentenced to the gallows.

The lawyer called on him in the death cell to present the bill for his services. Nothing had been said as to what the amount of the fee was to be, and now the attorney asked $10,000.

The condemned man just laughed at him. Afterward, the lawyer was telling an older attorney about the matter and concluded his narration with the question, "Do you think $10,000 an unreasonable fee for such a case?"

"Well," the veteran barrister said, cautiously, "I believe he could've been hung for less money."

A FARMER who had been seriously injured when he was struck by an automobile, employed a lawyer who gained a judgment in trial court for $1,000. The case was carried up through the various stages of appeal, but the plaintiff was successful and the Supreme Court upheld the judgment.

So the attorney, after the money had been collected, handed his client a five-dollar bill.

"What's this?" the farmer asked.

"That's all that was left after paying the various expenses and taking out my fee," the lawyer explained.

His client looked down at the five-dollar bill and inquired, "What's the matter with this? Is it counterfeit?"

☆　☆　☆　☆　☆　☆　☆

THE judge asked the defendant, "Are you guilty or not guilty?"

The accused man replied, "How can I tell till I've heard the evidence?"

☆　☆　☆　☆　☆　☆　☆

THE attorney was conducting a vigorous cross examination.

"Does Brown talk to himself when he's alone?"

The witness replied, "I don't know; I never was with him when he was alone."

☆　☆　☆　☆　☆　☆　☆

A LITTLE MAN stood before the bar of justice. He had a black eye and his face showed signs of punishment. His wife, a large woman, sat nearby; she had charged him with desertion.

"Your honor," said the prisoner's attorney, "this man is no deserter — he is a refugee."

☆　☆　☆　☆　☆　☆　☆

THE attorney demanded severely, "You testify that you saw the defendant strike the complaining witness, and yet you were three blocks away. How far can you see, anyhow?"

"Oh, I don't know," the witness drawled; "about a million miles, I expect — how far is the moon?"

☆　☆　☆　☆　☆　☆　☆

AN East Texas lawyer was sued and he decided to handle his own case. In due time, the lawsuit came to trial and at the conclusion of the testimony, he began his argument:

"Gentlemen of the jury, I know it is an old adage that the lawyer who conducts his own lawsuit hath a fool both for a client and an attorney."

He had to leave for Dallas while the jury was still out and he arranged with a friend to telegraph him the verdict. When he reached the hotel in Dallas, he found this telegram awaiting him, "Old adage unanimously upheld."

THE prisoner had sent for the town's leading criminal lawyer.

"Have you got anything in the way of cash for my fee?" the attorney wanted to know.

"No, but I've got a 1940 model Ford car."

"Well, that's fine. And what are you accused of?"

The prisoner replied, "Stealing a 1940 model Ford car."

☆ ☆ ☆ ☆ ☆ ☆ ☆

A FARMER, having employed a lawyer to handle a case for him, said: "I'll give you the facts and you can put in the lies to suit yourself."

☆ ☆ ☆ ☆ ☆ ☆ ☆

TWO RASCALS decided to rob a house in Houston one night. One entered the cottage while the other remained outside on watch. When the housebreaker returned, his comrade asked, "What luck?" The other said, "Nobody lives here but an old widow and she had only 36 cents, but I did as well as a lawyer could have done — I got all she had!"

☆ ☆ ☆ ☆ ☆ ☆ ☆

AT A banquet, a speaker proposed the toast, "An honest lawyer, the noblest work of God." Someone in the back of the hall added, "And about the rarest."

☆ ☆ ☆ ☆ ☆ ☆ ☆

OF COURSE, the oftenest-told joke along that line is the one about the man who read the inscription on a tombstone, "Here lies a lawyer and an honest man," and he remarked, "Ground must be scarce around here; they're burying them two to a grave."

☆ ☆ ☆ ☆ ☆ ☆ ☆

AND there is a similar story:

A visitor to a cemetery read the epitaph, "Here lies an honest lawyer" and he commented, "There's determination for you — he's dead and still lying."

☆ ☆ ☆ ☆ ☆ ☆ ☆

BUT the oldest of all the lawyer stories is the one about the man who called his lawyer on the telephone and explained matters to him. The attorney said, "They can't put you in jail for that."

His client replied, "Maybe not — but I'm talking from the jail now."

☆ ☆ ☆ ☆ ☆ ☆ ☆

THE newly-elected justice of the peace in the East Texas community had had no legal experience, but he had studied as best he could to qualify himself for his duties. At the conclusion of the testimony in his first trial, he said:

"The court will take this case under advisement until next Wednesday and will then decide in favor of the plaintiff."

HE WAS the same justice of the peace before whom a man was
brought for examining trial and the young county attorney said,
"Your honor, I stand ready to present three men who will testify
that they saw the prisoner chase the complaining witness with a
shotgun." The lawyer on the other side, veteran of years of
courtroom battles, declared, "And, your honor, I stand ready
to present nine men who will testify that they did not see the
prisoner chase this man with a shotgun." The squire stroked his
whiskers, then said, "Nine witnesses to three — that's the pre-
ponderance of the evidence; case dismissed!"

☆   ☆   ☆   ☆   ☆   ☆   ☆

AN OLD LAWYER was giving advice to a newly-admitted attorney:
"When the law is on your side and the facts are against you,
insist to the jury that justice be done though the heavens fall.
"If the facts are on your side but the law is against you, ask
what the world would be if it were not for mercy, for pity, for
the sympathetic feeling of man toward his fellow man."
The young lawyer asked, "But suppose both the law and the
facts are against me?"
"Then," the old-timer replied, "give the other side h——."

☆   ☆   ☆   ☆   ☆   ☆   ☆

THE defendant — we'll call him Pete Brown — stood up for the
reading of the indictment, and the district attorney started:
"The State of Texas versus Pete Brown ——"
Then the defendant broke in: "Hold up! Judge, does that
mean the whole State of Texas?"
"It does," said the judge.
"Then I plead guilty," said the defendant. "There's no use
of one man trying to fight 7,000,000 people."

☆   ☆   ☆   ☆   ☆   ☆   ☆

THE district attorney began a vigorous cross-examination of a
witness in a murder trial:
"Mr. Witness, you're not telling the same story now that
you did right after the shooting happened, are you?"
"No, sir."
"How do you explain this difference?"
"Well," the witness replied, "I was talkin' then; I'm swearin'
now."

☆   ☆   ☆   ☆   ☆   ☆   ☆

THE minister had begun the oration at the funeral of a lawyer
when a late arrival seated himself near the back and whispered
to an attorney, "How far along is it?" The other replied,
"They're just opening for the defense."

JUDGE BROWN — all West .Texas lawyers are called "judge" — was the leading attorney of the county; he had two outstanding characteristics — a strict adherence to the rules of evidence and an utter repugnance toward a personal difficulty.

One day, a citizen against whom he had filed suit, met him on the street and, anxious to provoke a fight so he could punch in the lawyer's face, said:

"You're a blankety-blank."

In a placating tone, Brown said, "Now, Henry, that's just your personal opinion in the matter."

☆　☆　☆　☆　☆　☆　☆

THE young lawyer had been appointed to represent the defendant. It was the attorney's first case and he decided to place the prisoner on the stand. The defendant was a hard-looking individual and was accused of burglary.

"Now, just tell the jury," said the attorney, "how many times you have been in jail."

"You mean in Texas?" asked the defendant.

(The jury gave him 14 years — the maximum sentence.)

☆　☆　☆　☆　☆　☆　☆

THE jury in a case on trial in Nacogdoches had been deliberating for hours and it was meal time, so the foreman called in the bailiff and said, "Order 11 suppers and a bale of hay."

☆　☆　☆　☆　☆　☆　☆

AND the Dallas Dispatch once came out with these two headlines over the main news stories:

"Bank robbers escape with $60,000";

"Attorneys receive $300,000 fee in estate lawsuit."

The reader may draw his own moral.

☆　☆　☆　☆　☆　☆　☆

JUSTICE OF THE PEACE ERNEST WOOD of Eastland relates this story of an early-day county judge who was a devout Baptist:

Some boys were brought before him on a charge of disturbing religious worship. After the evidence had been completed, he instructed the jury:

"Gentlemen of the jury, if you find from the evidence that it was a Baptist meeting, you will find each and all of the defendants guilty as charged.

"If you find, however, that it was a Methodist meeting, you will consider further of your verdict.

"But if you find that it was a Campbellite meeting, you will turn them all loose."

('Squire Wood belongs to the Christian church but relishes the story on his own denomination.)

"WHAT's your name?" demanded the mayor and ex officio city judge.

"John Smith," the prisoner replied.

"What's your right name?" shouted the judge.

"Henry Wadsworth Longfellow."

"That's more like it," the judge replied; "don't try that John Smith stuff on me."

☆ ☆ ☆ ☆ ☆ ☆ ☆

THE colored defendant was accused of chicken-stealing and the evidence was overwhelming. After the jury had brought in the verdict of "Guilty," the judge said to the prisoner:

"George, there's one thing about this case that I can't understand. How could you go into that backyard where there was a bulldog, force open the chicken house door, and go right past the window where the owner was asleep, with a whole sack of chickens, climb back over the fence and get away without arousing anyone?"

The negro said, "Jedge, ain't no use me 'splainin' to you; you couldn't do it."

☆ ☆ ☆ ☆ ☆ ☆ ☆

TOM PHILLIPS, of the Santa Rosa Signal, wrote that he attended a trial in justice court and one of the lawyers said to a witness:

"My good woman, you must give an answer in the fewest possible words of which you are capable, to the plain and simple question whether, when you were crossing the street with the baby on your arm, and that auto was coming down on the right side and the truck on the left side, and the motorcycle was trying to pass the auto, you saw the plaintiff between the motorcycle and the truck, or whether and when you saw him at all, and whether or not near the motorcycle, auto and truck, or either, or any two, and which of them respectively, or how was it."

☆ ☆ ☆ ☆ ☆ ☆ ☆

A DOWN-AND-OUTER stood before the small town justice of the peace on a charge of drunkenness. When asked if he had anything to say, the prisoner answered:

"Your honor, mine is an understandable weakness. Look at Edgar Allan Poe, half drunk when he wrote 'The Raven'; Bobbie Burns, lit up a large part of the time, and the same way with Lord Byron."

"That don't excuse you. You're fined $10 and costs. And, Mr. Constable, if you find any of them fellers he mentioned in my precinct, bring 'em in; we're goin' to have law an' order around here."

"DON'T you want a lawyer?" the judge asked the dusky defendant.

"Naw, suh, jedge," he replied, "I'll jes' throw mahself on de ignorance ob de co'rt."

☆   ☆   ☆   ☆   ☆   ☆   ☆

AN East Texas lawyer named Strange remarked that he did not want his name carved on his tombstone, but simply, "Here lies a lawyer and an honest man," as everyone who read it would exclaim, "That's Strange!"

☆   ☆   ☆   ☆   ☆   ☆   ☆

IN THE old days when a man applied for admission to the bar, he was examined by a committee of local lawyers and they were as easy as possible, but in one instance they were having a difficult time of it. They had asked several simple questions, but the applicant was utterly unable to answer even one of them. At last, the chairman inquired:

"Have you studied Greenleaf on Evidence?"

"No, judge."

"Or Blackstone's Commentaries?"

"No, sir."

"Well, have you read anything whatever on law?"

"Yes, sir — I've read a good deal of a book called the Statutes of Texas."

The lawyer replied, "Young man, the trouble with that is the next legislature is liable to meet and repeal all the law you know."

☆   ☆   ☆   ☆   ☆   ☆   ☆

OIL FIELD MAXIM: A gusher clouds a title; a dry hole clears it.

☆   ☆   ☆   ☆   ☆   ☆   ☆

THE boy had never been in court before and so, as he sat in the witness chair, he answered the district attorney's questions in such a low tone that the official said, "Speak up so those gentlemen over there in the jury box can hear you."

"Oh!" exclaimed the lad as his countenance lighted up, "are those men interested in this case, too?"

☆   ☆   ☆   ☆   ☆   ☆   ☆

WHENEVER Judge Roy Bean was trying a homicide case, he is said always to have told the jury, "The first question is: Should the deceased have departed?"

Texas at War

HERE's a little jingle from the San Saba Star:
  You can tell an apprentice seaman by his look of great alarm;
  You can tell a petty officer by the chevrons on his arm;
  You can tell a lieutenant by his manners, dress and such;
  You can also tell an ensign—but you can't tell him very much.

☆ ☆ ☆ ☆ ☆ ☆ ☆

SEVERAL Army brides were talking about their husbands.

The first one remarked that her husband, who had been a captain, had obtained his majority.

The second one said: "Bill has just received notice of his captaincy"; while the third remarked that her husband was hoping for a first lieutenancy soon.

The fourth wife, feeling that she was called upon to say something, declared: "Well, Johnny still has his privacy, anyway."

A RECRUITING OFFICER asked a colored applicant, "Have you had any previous experience?" He replied, "I sho' has, boss; I'se been shot at three times befo' dere evah wuz a wah!"

☆   ☆   ☆   ☆   ☆   ☆   ☆

THE sergeant sent the recruit from New York's East Side to saddle and bridle a horse. When the man had not returned after half an hour, the sergeant went to look for him and found him standing near a horse and holding the bridle.

"Why don't you put it in his mouth?" the sergeant demanded.

"I'm waitin' for him to yawn," replied the rookie.

☆   ☆   ☆   ☆   ☆   ☆   ☆

THE two darkeys were under fire for the first time.

One said, "Ah sho is nervous."

His buddie replied, "There's nothin' to be skeered of; you ain't gonna get hit 'less one of dem bullets has yoah name on it."

The first one rejoined, "Ah ain't afraid ob a bullet wid my name on it; it's a bullet that is addressed, 'To Whom It May Concern' dat I'se worried about."

☆   ☆   ☆   ☆   ☆   ☆   ☆

A TEXAS army camp was commanded by Colonel Berry. One night, his wife and daughter were challenged by the sentry, and he refused to admit them.

"But," protested the wife, "we are the Berrys."

"I don't care if you're the cat's whiskers; you can't get in without the password," the sentinel replied.

☆   ☆   ☆   ☆   ☆   ☆   ☆

A VISITOR to the encampment said to a soldier, "I'd like to see someone with a little authority." He replied, "Well, I'm a private and have about as little authority as anybody I know."

☆   ☆   ☆   ☆   ☆   ☆   ☆

AN East Texas soldier, newly-arrived in France, made a purchase and thought he had been short-changed. He looked around and saw another Texan, whom he asked, "How long you been over here?"

The other said, "Three months."

"Can you speak French?"

"Like a native."

So the East Texan explained the situation, and his buddy entered the shop and said to the shop-keeper, "Parley-voo fransay?"

"Oui, oui, m'sier," replied the Frenchman.

"Then," yelled the soldier, "why in h—— don't you give my friend the rest of his change?"

MILITARY LIFE had broadened his shoulders, put sparkle into his eyes, bronzed and tanned his face behind the set of whiskers that he had grown while on a South Sea island, so that his mother did not know him when he returned on a furlough. At last, however, when he sat down to the table, she recognized him — recognized him by his appetite!

☆　☆　☆　☆　☆　☆　☆

TWO RECRUITS were talking. One said, "I feel like punching the sergeant in the nose again." The other one exclaimed, "Again?"

"Yes — I felt like it yesterday, too."

☆　☆　☆　☆　☆　☆　☆

A TEXAS VETERAN was telling about his experiences in Paris during the war.

"Did you buy any eau de cologne?" a friend asked.

"I wanted to but I couldn't think of the French for it," he replied.

☆　☆　☆　☆　☆　☆　☆

DURING the "gas" shortage occasioned by World War II, a Texas motorist read the advertisement of a "gasoline saver" that would save sixty per cent of the gasoline, then he read the ad of another that would save seventy per cent. So he equipped his car with both — and began manufacturing gasoline.

☆　☆　☆　☆　☆　☆　☆

THE sergeant had been something of a hand at having a fight or two on Saturday nights when he went into town after a week of cow-punching back in Texas — but now the shells were whistling around. He remarked to his companion in a fox-hole:

"Bud, when I get back home, the only thing I'll ever be arrested for is singing too loud in church!"

☆　☆　☆　☆　☆　☆　☆

THE negro sergeant was giving his first talk to a bunch of rookies:

"When dat bugle sounds tomorrow mornin', Ah wants to see clouds of dust boilin' outta dem tents and when de clouds settle, Ah wants to see two rows ob immovable statues."

☆　☆　☆　☆　☆　☆　☆

A RECRUIT from Brooklyn went out for a walk around the camp and came back displaying a set of rattles.

"Where did you get them?" a buddy asked.

"I took 'em off a big woim," he replied.

☆　☆　☆　☆　☆　☆　☆

OLDEST of all the war jokes:

The regiment was parading through the town and a proud mother said to a friend, "Look, Sally; they're all out of step but Jim."

A VARIANT:

The sergeant approached a rookie and said, sarcastically, "Do you know that everybody is outta step except you?"

The soldier replied, "Well, you tell 'em; you're the sergeant."

☆ ☆ ☆ ☆ ☆ ☆ ☆

THE major general was challenged by a rookie sentry.

"I've forgotten the password, but I'm the commanding officer of this camp," the general said.

"Can't let anybody in without the password," was the reply of the unimpressed soldier.

"But I'm a major general," said the officer, in exasperation. "Look at these stars on my shoulder; do you know what they mean?"

"Yeah," said the private, "they mean you got two sons in the service."

☆ ☆ ☆ ☆ ☆ ☆ ☆

IN EARLY DAYS, the general in command of the string of Texas frontier forts wished to impress the red men with the impossibility of defeating the whites. So he called in an old wilderness scout and said:

"I want you to tell the Indians that the white man builds boats that will carry a hundred men."

The scout replied, "I'll tell 'em but they won't believe it."

"And," the general continued, "tell them that the palefaces have iron horses that will carry 200 men."

"I'll tell 'em," the other said, "but they won't believe it."

"And," directed the general, "tell them I can touch this key" — and he pointed to a telegraph instrument — "and talk to the Great White Father in Washington."

"Thunder," the old fellow exclaimed, "I don't believe that myself!"

☆ ☆ ☆ ☆ ☆ ☆ ☆

PYOTE, TEXAS
By Pfc. Ed Koops

I REMEMBER so well the day I came to Pyote. I was dozing in the day-coach, dreaming up a pleasant little plot about Texas, the Law West of the Pecos, and me, my pony and my guitar!

I was ridin' herd on a bunch of cattle rustlers who had made off with a young miss. I had just traced them to their hideout, where they were torturing that lovely young miss — when the conductor woke me up. And I saw Pyote!

It was then and there that I decided to sign a separate peace with the Axis and go home quietly.

I got off the train and saw the town. Nothing! Nothing at all!

(It appeared I was facing the wrong way; I turned around). Then I saw it — the Blank Cafe, the Only One of Its Kind — I thanked God for that small favor.

Just then a great brown cloud appeared in the sky. It whooshed its way toward me, a juggernaut whipping into its maelstrom telephone poles, filling stations and the right wing of the T. & P. Railroad. It hit!

Two weeks later, I arrived back in Pyote, footsore and weary. That, we were later to discover, was one of the soft spring zephyrs that blow through West Texas.

The beds! There's so much sand in them, it's like sleeping in a bag of gravel. It's . . . sh-sh . . . dust. (No loyal Texan will admit that it's dust). We shall play it safe and say that every evening the land of Oklahoma drops in for a visit and blows back the next day. But it drops so often!

We don't need furloughs here; no, sir, you just wait long enough and the whole U.S. — grain by grain — flits right down on the barracks floor.

We had the foolish nerve to approach a Native of Texas — you can recognize these Natives: they have a Lone Star branded on their foreheads, spit to the windward and have the foolish idea that we d—— yankees are down here because we like it. I went up to one of them and said:

"Hey, why doncha do somepin' about the dust?"

Well, I must admit that he was courteous about it. And besides I never used that eye much, anyway.

All they say about the dust is, "It's clean." Yup, it doesn't stay in one place long enough to get dirty.

Then you want a big evening with bright lights, song, laughter, wine, and you hit the trail to Monahans. The only difference between Monahans and Pyote is that Monahans is on both sides of the street.

Pyote? Well, just picture a ghost town, multiply it by Sodom and Gomorrah after the retribution, add the scorched earth policy, and you have some conception of it.

It's the only town in the U.S.A. that uses the sign, "You are now entering Pyote," and on the other side of the same sign, "You are now leaving Pyote."

"Cullud Folks"

"I GOT a gal dat weighs 250 pounds," Ham said, "an' last night I held her on my knee fer two hours."

"Lawsy!" exclaimed his friend.

"Yas, sah," Ham continued, "de fust hour I wuz hypnotized an' de second hour I wuz paralyzed."

☆   ☆   ☆   ☆   ☆   ☆   ☆

THE two darkeys sat down in the shade near the factory, where they were employed, to eat lunch. Alex opened his lunch box and produced a queer-looking object.

"Whut is dat?" Sam wanted to know.

"Dat's a thermos bottle," Alex explained. "My wife kin put coffee in dar an' it'll stay hot all mawnin', or she kin put tea in dar an' it'll stay cold all mawnin'."

"It show is wunnerful," said Sam, in an awestruck tone, "but how do it know which to do?"

66

THE two colored men had not seen each other for a good many years. One asked, "How's yore wife?"

The other said, "Mah wife am an angel."

The first one remarked, "You sho' is lucky; mine's still livin'."

☆ ☆ ☆ ☆ ☆ ☆ ☆

"HELP! help!" shouted a black lad who had been fishing when he fell into the river.

Unhesitatingly, a negro man leaped into the cold water, seized the boy and dragged him to shore. Several white men ran up and congratulated the man on his heroism.

"Is he your son?" one asked.

"Naw, suh."

"Your nephew, then?"

"Naw, suh, he ain't no kin to me."

"And yet you unhesitatingly leaped into the cold, swift current of this river to save him."

"Well, boss," the hero explained, "he had de bait in his pocket."

☆ ☆ ☆ ☆ ☆ ☆ ☆

MOSE had been found guilty of murder in the first degree and the judge ordered him to stand:

"I sentence you to death in the electric chair on May 15."

The negro turned ashy pale and stammered:

"Jedge, does you mean dis comin' May?"

☆ ☆ ☆ ☆ ☆ ☆ ☆

TWO NEGROES were arguing angrily and one of them said, "Where I comes from, dat word means fight." The other squared his shoulders and asked, "Den why don't you fight?" The first one replied, "Because I ain't where I comes from."

☆ ☆ ☆ ☆ ☆ ☆ ☆

THE colored parson was found embracing one of the sisters of the congregation. The board summoned him before them but he defended himself with Scripture: "Doan it say in de Book dat de shepherd taketh de lambs unto his bosom?" The deacons deliberated, and then passed the following motion, "Be it resolved, dat we keeps Bruddah Jones as pastor but dat, in de future, when he taketh a lamb unto his bosom, it shall be a ram lamb."

☆ ☆ ☆ ☆ ☆ ☆ ☆

"NIGGAH, Ford dem dice!"

"Whut do you mean — Ford dem dice?"

"Shake, rattle and roll."

☆ ☆ ☆ ☆ ☆ ☆ ☆

THE exhorter announced, "Mah subject am Sin — an' I am full o' my subject."

A BASEBALL GAME was in progress and a big negro strode up to the plate. At the first pitch, the little negro who was umpiring said, "Strike one."

The batter turned and scowled. After the next pitch, the umpire called, "Ball one."

On the third pitch, he said, "Two."

"Two whut?" demanded the husky batsman.

"Too high," the umpire replied.

☆　☆　☆　☆　☆　☆　☆

THERE was another negro baseball game — this one was being played at Huntsville between teams of convicts. The bases were full, and nobody was out, and from the sidelines rose a plea to the pitcher, "Big boy, take yoah time; youse got eighteen yeahs!"

☆　☆　☆　☆　☆　☆　☆

"UNCLE JOE, how did you come out on your crop this year?"

"Why, Kunn'l, de ducks got it."

"The ducks — what do you mean?"

"Well, de storekeeper he say, de duck fer de groceries, an' de ginner he say, de duck fer de ginnin', and de landlord he say, de duck fer de rent — yes, suh, de ducks got it all."

☆　☆　☆　☆　☆　☆　☆

A MOB had just finished lynching a negro. He had been hanged; then his body was cut down and burned; and while the fire was still going, a few shots were fired into the body.

Just then an old darkey came along and somebody growled, "Maybe we ought to string him up, too."

Someone else demanded, "I guess you disapprove of what we've done?"

The old fellow stammered, "Naw, suh, it looks to me lak he got off mighty light."

☆　☆　☆　☆　☆　☆　☆

THE banker grew weary of "lending" Sam two-bits every few days, and so he suggested, "Why don't you go to work?"

"I'd be glad to," the negro replied, "but I don't know of no jobs."

"You could get a job at the Eagle Laundry," said the banker.

Sam looked uneasy and then said, "Cunn'l, I ain't had no experience launderin' no eagles."

☆　☆　☆　☆　☆　☆　☆

"MAH SUBJECT tonight am Liahs," said the parson. "How many ob you-all has read the eleventh chapter of Fifth Corinthians?"

Hands shot up over the house.

"You-all am de ones Ah'm gonna preach 'specially to — 'cause dar ain't no Fifth Corinthians," said Preacher Brown.

MANDY couldn't read or write, so when she signed the payroll, she made an "X." One day, however, she made an "O" and when she was asked why, she replied:

"I done changed my name; I'se got married."

☆   ☆   ☆   ☆   ☆   ☆   ☆

"How is it that we never hear of a negro committing suicide?" a visitor from the North inquired of Uncle Henry.

"Well, suh, hits lak dis," the old darkey replied. "When a white man gits to worryin' about somethin', he sets down an' keeps on worryin' an' worryin' an' finally ups an' kills hisself. But when one ob us gits to worryin' an' sets down, purty soon we goes to sleep.

"An', o' course, when we wakes up, we'se done fo'got whut we wuz worryin' about."

☆   ☆   ☆   ☆   ☆   ☆   ☆

THE two negroes were good friends — and neither of them could read. One day, Rastus received a telegram. He tore it open, glanced at it, and handing it to the other, said:

"Dar it am."

The other looked at it and said:

"Durned ef it ain't."

☆   ☆   ☆   ☆   ☆   ☆   ☆

EVERY TIME Jeff asked the doctor, "How is mah wife gittin' along?" the physician would reply, "She is improving" — but one night she died.

Next day, a friend asked the bereaved husband, "What did she die from?"

"From improvements," he replied.

☆   ☆   ☆   ☆   ☆   ☆   ☆

A DARKEY was telling about the death of his grandmother, age 98.

"What caused her death?" someone inquired.

"Nothin' serious," was the answer.

☆   ☆   ☆   ☆   ☆   ☆   ☆

THE man had plenty of money but had the reputation of being the tightest fellow in town. He was the kind the bankers call judiciously thrifty.

One morning, he was standing on the corner in front of the bank when he was approached by an old negro who had known him for 50 years, and who now wanted a "two-bit" loan.

The close-fisted fellow started ransacking his pockets, and made as if he didn't have the money.

"Well, Sam," he said, "I thought I had a quarter this morning but I don't seem to find it."

"Please look again, suh," urged the negro, "for if you had one this mawnin', you still got it."

SAMBO was on trial and the judge said: "You are accused of stealing chickens. Do you have any witnesses?"

"Naw, suh, jedge," the prisoner responded. "When I steals chickens, I don't have no witnesses."

☆　☆　☆　☆　☆　☆　☆

AN "AUNTY" approached the ticket window and said, "Ah wants a ticket fer Virginny."

The agent inquired, "What part of Virginia?"

"All of Virginny," was the answer; "dat's Virginny sittin' on dat suitcase."

☆　☆　☆　☆　☆　☆　☆

A FEW of the very oldest ones:

I

A negro who was a witness in a trial for attempted murder was asked, "Did you hear the bullet?"

He replied, "Yas, suh, I heered it twict; once when it passed me and again when I passed it."

II

Similar was the testimony of a darkey who took to his heels when shooting began. A rabbit sprang out of the brush and went racing up the path ahead of him. The negro said, "Git outta de way an' let somebody run whut kin run."

III

A negro woman living over in the swamps near the Louisiana line rushed into the cabin and said to her husband:

"An alligator has jes' grabbed little Willie."

He replied, "You know, I thought somethin' had been gittin' ouah chillun."

IV

A darkey joining the Army was asked if he wanted to go into the cavalry.

"Naw, suh," he said, "in case of a battle, I don't want to be bothered wid no hoss."

V

"Can you change a $10-bill, Uncle?" said a white man to an aged darkey.

"Naw, suh," he answered, "but thanks fur de compliment."

☆　☆　☆　☆　☆　☆　☆

TWO NEGROES were playing poker.

"Whut you got?" asked one.

"Fo' kings," replied the other, "an' whut has you got?"

"Two sixes an' a razor."

The other said, "Boy, how come you so lucky?"

A NEGRO newly arrived at Huntsville was placed in a cell with another member of his race. The newcomer asked, "Whut you in fer?"

"Murdah," was the reply.

"How long you gonna be here?"

"Three weeks."

"Dat ain't jestice!" exclaimed the other prisoner. "I jes' stole an automobile an' dey give me three yeahs."

"Yeah," the killer said, "I is heah only three weeks an' den dey hangs me."

☆　　☆　　☆　　☆　　☆　　☆　　☆

COLORED exhorters are never stumped by questions pertaining to Holy Writ.

"Pahson, what wuz de epistles?" asked a feminine member of the congregation.

"De epistles, sistah, wuz de wives ob de apostles," the minister replied.

☆　　☆　　☆　　☆　　☆　　☆　　☆

UNCLE RASTUS had often told his young nieces and nephews about the wonders of Mollie Bailey's Circus, the attraction which for years visited the smaller towns of Texas.

"Hit's de greatest circus in de world," Rastus would declare.

But one day, while in Palestine, young Sam led him to a huge poster advertising Ringling Bros. Circus, which was coming to town on Sept. 1. In great, red type, the poster proclaimed, "Greatest Show on Earth."

"How come?" the nephew asked. "I thought you say Mollie Bailey's was de biggest."

The old man slowly spelled out the words, "Ringling Bros. Circus, Greatest Show on Earth, S-E-P-T 1." Then his face brightened as he repeated, " 'sept one" and he added, "An' dat one is Mollie Bailey's."

☆　　☆　　☆　　☆　　☆　　☆　　☆

THE new preacher had had a rather checkered past. One morning as he arose to begin his sermon, he was horrified to see in a seat near the door one who had been his cell-mate in the penitentiary. The parson gasped, but quickly recovered himself and said:

"Bred'ren, dis mawnin' Ah takes fuh my text de Scriptuah, he who recognizes me an' sayeth nothin, him will Ah see afterwa'd."

A NEGRO was complaining to a friend about the numerous rats that were overrunning his home. The friend said, "You ought to get some Rat Biscuits." The other heatedly answered, "If them rats is too good to eat whut we eats, to h—— wid 'em!"

☆ ☆ ☆ ☆ ☆ ☆ ☆

SAMBO was taking his first plane ride — a hop above an airport. The pilot put the ship through a flock of maneuvers, including some thrilling dips and spins, then straightened out and yelled to his lone passenger:

"I'll bet fifty per cent of the people down there thought we were falling then."

The darky replied:

"Yas suh — an' fifty per cent of dem up heah thought de same thing!"

☆ ☆ ☆ ☆ ☆ ☆ ☆

A COLORED MAID said to the lady for whom she worked, "Trouble am so high dat you can't climb it, so wide you can't walk around it, so deep you can't dig undah it — so de only way to beat it am jes' to duck youah haid an' wade right through it!"

☆ ☆ ☆ ☆ ☆ ☆ ☆

A COLORED PARSON found one of his members shooting craps on the Sabbath and rebuked him: "Doan you know it am a sin to gamble on Sunday?"

The other replied, "Yas, pahson, an' I shore is payin' for mah sin."

A MAN entered a hole-in-the-wall eating place in Waco and a scowling waiter growled, "What can I give you?" The customer said, "Two scrambled eggs and some kind words."

The waiter returned in a little while and said, "Here's your eggs."

"How about the kind words?"

The waiter replied, "Don't eat them eggs."

☆ ☆ ☆ ☆ ☆ ☆ ☆

A LONESOME telegraph operator in a little sand-and-cactus town adopted a rattlesnake as a pet and, to while away the time, the telegrapher taught the creature to rattle the Morse code.

The Smell of Printer's Ink

A TRAMP PRINTER got off a freight train and applied for a job at the Weekly Bugle. The editor handed him two pieces of "copy" — an account of a wedding and a farmer's auction sale announcement. The printer got hold of a jug of whiskey, with the following result:

"William Smith and Lucy Jones were disposed of at public auction at my farm one mile east of a beautiful cluster of roses and two white calves before a background of farm implements too numerous to mention in the presence of about sixty guests including two milch cows, six mules and one wagon. Rev. Jackson tied the nuptial knot, with about 200 feet of hay rope and the bridal party left on one good John Deere gang plow for an extended trip with terms to suit purchasers."

An EDITOR in a Texas town was explaining how he whipped an indignant subscriber, and in the telling made large use of the editorial "we." Here is what he wrote:

"There was a blow; somebody fell. We got up. Turning on our antagonist, we succeeded in winding his arms around our waist and, by a quick maneuver, threw him on top of us, bringing our back at the same time in contact with the solid bed of the printing press. Then, inserting our nose between his teeth and cleverly entangling his hands in our hair, we had him."

☆ ☆ ☆ ☆ ☆ ☆ ☆

THE towel in the old-time printing office saw much service and often it was heavily encrusted in grime and printer's ink. One day, two typesetters had a quarrel, and one stabbed the other to death with the towel.

☆ ☆ ☆ ☆ ☆ ☆ ☆

THE copy-desk man was busy with an article that consisted of half a dozen pages. A visitor asked, "What are you doing, Joe?"

He replied, "I'm editing the president's message."

His friend said, "Do you mean to say that you, a $40-a-week man, are editing the message of the President of the United States?"

"H——, yes," the other answered, "and I'd edit the Sermon on the Mount if I found a split infinitive in it."

☆ ☆ ☆ ☆ ☆ ☆ ☆

THE old editor of the small-town daily was ill one day and his young assistant got out the paper. The biggest event of the day was a fist-fight and the acting editor "bannered" on it, using 144-point type, which is two inches high, for the headline.

Next day, the veteran journalist was back on the job, and the assistant kept waiting for some comment on his work. None being forthcoming, at last he asked, "What did you think of yesterday's paper?"

The old-timer said, "Oh, it was all right, but I was saving that type for the Second Coming of Jesus Christ."

☆ ☆ ☆ ☆ ☆ ☆ ☆

AN old-time one (not true in these days of up-to-date, money-making methods in the operation of small-town newspapers):

The editor of a home town weekly retired with a fortune, and he gave this as the recipe of his success:

"I attribute the fact that I have been able to accumulate $100,000 to the fact that I worked hard and long, that I was thrifty and economical and practiced a policy of strict honesty, and to having an uncle who died, leaving me $97,000."

THE editor of a country town weekly wrote a news item about a Civil War veteran, back in the 20's during prohibition days. He used the phrase, "the battle-scarred veteran," but it came out in the paper, "the bottle-scarred veteran."

He attempted a correction the next week, and that time it came out: "the battle-scared veteran."

So the editor left town on the next train.

☆　☆　☆　☆　☆　☆　☆

A MODEL VISITOR to a newspaper office was described in "Texas Siftings":

He did not put his feet upon the table and tamper with the exchanges. He did not give us a mile and a half of advice how to make the paper popular with the masses. This alone made us look on him in the light of a sainted angel.

He did not startle us with a new joke that he claimed to have originated last week but which we remembered to have heard in a circus thirty years ago.

Neither did he tell us anything about his having shot a deer, away back in 1840, on the spot where the capitol now stands.

☆　☆　☆　☆　☆　☆　☆

"NAMES make news," the state editor advised a small-town correspondent. A few days later, the correspondent sent in this item:

"Fire last night destroyed Farmer Huck Jones' barn and claimed the lives of three cows, named Bossy, Bessy and Rosy."

☆　☆　☆　☆　☆　☆　☆

THE heading, "Births, Marriages, Deaths," is a standing one on many papers. One Texas editor, however, used the heading, "Yells, Bells and Knells."

And another headed the department, "Hatched, Matched and Snatched."

☆　☆　☆　☆　☆　☆　☆

THE ace writer of a metropolitan paper was dispatched to the Central Texas oil field to cover the story of a flaming well that had claimed a dozen lives. His instructions were to hold his account to a thousand words. He wired:

"Story so tremendous impossible to tell in less than 2,000 words."

An unfeeling managing editor telegraphed back:

"Creation of world and making of man told in Genesis in 600 words; the limit of your story is still 1,000 words."

☆　☆　☆　☆　☆　☆　☆

A WANT AD which appeared in a Texas newspaper:

"If John Blank, who deserted his wife and baby 21 years ago, will return, said baby will knock h—— out of him."

ANOTHER AD:

"To whom it may concern: I am not responsible for my wife's debts — or my own, either."

☆　☆　☆　☆　☆　☆　☆

THEN there was a staff writer who was sent to record an out-of-town murder trial. He got "lit up" and so one of the other correspondents, being a good friend, wrote a story, signed the incapacitated one's name and had it telegraphed to the other's paper.

Next day, the sobering one received a message from the editor:

"When you decide to get drunk again, designate one of your friends to write your story for you — received five stories last night signed by you."

☆　☆　☆　☆　☆　☆　☆

THE visitor flourished a copy of that day's paper in his hand and bellowed to the editor: "See here, I'm not dead but your paper says I am. I demand a retraction!"

The editor replied, "The Herald can never admit it made a mistake, but I'll tell what we'll do — we'll put your name in the birth column tomorrow and give you a fresh start."

☆　☆　☆　☆　☆　☆　☆

Two colored business men dissolved partnership and then Mose placed this notice in the paper:

"The partnership heretofore existing between Mose Brown and Lige Jones is hereby dissolved. Them what owes the firm will see Mose; them what the firm owes will see Lige."

☆　☆　☆　☆　☆　☆　☆

OLDEST of all the newspaper tales:

A "cub" was assigned to write up a fashionable church wedding. He returned to the office and seated himself at his typewriter, but when he did not start writing, the city editor came over and said:

"Where's the story?"

The reporter replied, "There ain't no story — the bridegroom didn't show up."

☆　☆　☆　☆　☆　☆　☆

THE reporter was all right when it came to getting the facts, but he was sometimes only approximate in the use of words. One day, the torso of a woman was found under an abandoned house. When he came in, he asked the city editor:

"What's this I hear about a woman's trousseau being found under a house?"

THIS reporter couldn't spell, either. He wrote a story about the towns affiliated with the West Texas Chamber of Commerce and those not so affiliated. Only he listed them as "Towns afflicted with the West Texas Chamber of Commerce" and "Towns not afflicted with the West Texas Chamber of Commerce."

☆   ☆   ☆   ☆   ☆   ☆   ☆

THERE had been a mine disaster in the coal district of West Texas, so the metropolitan paper assigned the star writer to "cover" the tragedy. It was time for his story to come ticking over the wire, and at last the telegrapher signaled the waiting group that it was coming. The "lead" was:

"Almighty God sits in judgment tonight on the hills overlooking Thurber."

The managing editor yelled to the telegraph operator, "Break in; send him this message: Never mind mine disaster; interview God."

☆   ☆   ☆   ☆   ☆   ☆   ☆

A TYPOGRAPHICAL ERROR crept into an account of the flower show:

"Mr. Jones attracted much attention by the large red nose which he displayed. Years of careful cultivation were necessary to produce an exhibit of such brilliance."

☆   ☆   ☆   ☆   ☆   ☆   ☆

THE new editor was a crusader and one day the paper came out with the headline, "Half the City Council Are Rascals."

There was a great outcry from the city hall, with threats, so the editor promised to make amends next day. And the issue the following afternoon carried the headline, "Half the City Council Are Not Rascals."

☆   ☆   ☆   ☆   ☆   ☆   ☆

THE new reporter on a Fort Worth daily turned in an article in which he referred to a "local school teacher." The head of the copy desk said, "Son, always use the name of the city; never use the word 'local.' "

Later, the reporter turned in a writeup of an operation undergone by a well-known man and included this detail:

"The surgeon used a Fort Worth anesthetic."

☆   ☆   ☆   ☆   ☆   ☆   ☆

THE same paper has a rule against using "evening" on the ground that "night" is the more exact term. A new reporter, anxious to comply with instructions, wrote in an account of a fashionable party:

"The hostess was lovely in a pink silk night gown."

"NEVER state anything as a fact that you do not know of your own personal knowledge," the city editor instructed the cub reporter.

With that instruction in mind, the youth turned in the following writeup:

"A woman giving the name of Mrs. James Jones, who is reported to be one of the society leaders of the city, is said to have given what purported to be a party yesterday to a number of alleged ladies. The hostess claims to be the wife of a reputed attorney."

☆   ☆   ☆   ☆   ☆   ☆   ☆

RAIN is just about the biggest news that can happen in West Texas. But one night the news editor had a problem: there had been a heavy, general rain accompanied by several fatalities. He solved the situation with this headline:

"Beneficial Rains Drown 7 In West Texas."

☆   ☆   ☆   ☆   ☆   ☆   ☆

"NOISY" HOLMES — that's near enough to his correct name — was well, if not favorably, known in the oil boom town.

One night his car overturned and he was pinned beneath the machine. As approaching motorists slowed down, then saw who it was, they sped on, thinking it was a trap to cause them to stop so they would be robbed.

Holmes grew desperate and, remembering he had $600 in a hip pocket, managed to get the money out and wave it in the beams of the next car's headlights. The driver, figuring that no one would be rash enough to display so much money in the oil field unless the situation was grave, stopped and carried the injured man to the hospital.

The Times' reporter learned of the incident and wrote it up, referring to Holmes as "an oil field character."

When that worthy recovered, he went around to the newspaper office to give the reporter a licking.

"But why?" the news-gatherer asked, stalling for time.

"You insulted me — you called me a character" was the reply.

Knowing that Holmes' education was limited, the reporter said, "Mr. Holmes, do you know exactly what that word means?"

"Well, no," he conceded, "I don't."

"Then, let's see what the dictionary says," and the newspaperman opened Mr. Webster's volume and read: "Character — nobility of purpose, loftiness of mind and achievement."

"By George," Noisy exclaimed, "I been complimented! Let me have six of them papers — I want to mail them to my folks back in Oklahoma."

THE editor's little girl attended Sunday School for the first time and returned with a small card on which was a verse of Scripture. "What do you have?" her mother asked. "Oh," little Susie replied, "just an ad about heaven."

☆   ☆   ☆   ☆   ☆   ☆   ☆

THE only business that can make money without advertising is the mint.

☆   ☆   ☆   ☆   ☆   ☆   ☆

THE editor was mailing back a poetic atrocity, entitled "Why Do I Live?" He scrawled, "Because you sent this instead of bringing it in person."

☆   ☆   ☆   ☆   ☆   ☆   ☆

A TELEPHONE rang and the city editor answered. An excited voice said, "Is this the Daily Bugle?" "Yes," was the reply.

"Well, I thought you would be interested in something that just now happened at the City Hospital; a baby was born about half an hour ago and its body from the waist down is black."

Excitedly, the city editor said, "I certainly want to thank you, because that is surely interesting, if it is true."

"It's true, all right," the informant insisted.

"What color is the baby's body from the waist up?" asked the newspaperman.

"Black" — and there was the click of a receiver being hung up.

☆   ☆   ☆   ☆   ☆   ☆   ☆

WHEN the first real cold weather hits, folks butcher hogs. So the reporter began a "weather story" thus:

"Tomorrow will be hog-killing weather."

The headline writer, who was newly arrived from New York City, headed the item, "Farmers, Protect Your Hogs."

☆   ☆   ☆   ☆   ☆   ☆   ☆

A TEXAS EDITOR burst into lyrical rapture, not on spring, beautiful spring, but on autumn:

> "The autumn leaves are falling;
>   They are falling all around;
> They are falling upon the earth,
>   And also on the ground."

"State Press" in the Dallas News added a verse:

> "The autumn leaves are falling;
>   They are falling everywhere;
> They are falling through the atmosphere,
>   And also through the air."

Vignettes

THE MAN WHO GOT ONE VOTE

THERE was a man in a West Texas town a long time ago (before the days of woman's suffrage) who detected a great public demand for him to run for office.

Now Joe had seven brothers-in-law and he, and they did not get along very well together. Nevertheless, he told them of his decision:

"The present town marshal has been in office a long time; things are ripe for a change and this is my opportunity."

Each of the seven did his best to discourage Joe, but he ascribed their counsel to envy for one who was about to sit in the seats of the mighty and taste the fruits of power.

When the brothers-in-law perceived that he was determined to make the race regardless of their advice, each assured him:

"I don't think you are doing the wise thing but you can count on me."

Joe made a thorough canvass. For weeks, he handed out cards and shook hands. He attended barbecues by day and pie suppers by night; he rejoiced at the wedding feasts and he mourned with stricken families at the grave.

Election day rolled around. That night, the count showed 412 for the old marshal and exactly one vote for Joe.

Next morning, an acquaintance met the recent candidate on the street and sought to sympathize with him:

"I was for the other fellow, but I'm sorry you got only one vote."

Joe replied, "Well, it could've been worse; I might've got two votes."

The other was mystified, "How do you figure getting two votes would be worse than getting only one?"

"Well, it's like this," Joe explained. "I know who cast that one vote — I did, myself. If I had received two votes, each of my seven brothers-in-law would've sworn that he cast that other vote.

"But, as it is, I know durn well that not one of the dirty bums voted for me and so I'm going to lick h—— out o' them, one right after the other."

Which he did.

☆ ☆ ☆ ☆ ☆ ☆ ☆

$100-A-DAY HOTEL SUITE

WHILE "Farmer Jim" Ferguson was serving his first term as Governor, he made a trip to New York City on a matter of official business and put up at the Waldorf-Astoria in a suite that cost $100 a day, his long-time friend and political associate, Fisher Alsup recalls. When Ferguson was asking re-election, opposition speakers made much of the $100-a-day hotel suite. The governor ignored the matter until the campaign was rather well along, and then at Hillsboro a heckler broke into his speech with the cry, "How about that New York trip?"

"My friends," (said Governor Jim, as Alsup reconstructs the speech) "I am a native Texan. My father died when I was three years old and I was raised by a widowed mother on Salado Creek, about eight miles south of the little county seat town of Belton.

"We had our land and some stock but very little else, and I have cut those Spanish oak saplings into stovewood and hauled it into Belton in my late teens and sold it for $2.50 a wagonload.

"There are men in this crowd who have seen me come into town with a wagon-sheet over a load of wood, with fodder for my horses and a little meat along for my own food, and if I got into Belton too late to sell the load of wood that afternoon, I spent the night in the wagon yard and then next morning, after disposing of the load, I would buy a little flour, sugar and coffee, then return to my home.

"I make no apologies for having stayed at the wagon yard because that was in keeping with my station in life, and I was representing no one but Jim Ferguson, and my poverty and misfortunes meant nothing to anyone else.

"But when I went to New York City, I was there as governor of the State of Texas on official business; I went there representing a proud people, a wealthy people, a citizenship that is not satisfied with anything but the best. And I didn't put up at the wagon yard. I went to the finest hotel and I paid $100 a day for a suite, and the only reason I didn't spend $200 a day was they didn't have one that cost that much!"

The reply was so devastating that the opposition never mentioned the matter again.

☆   ☆   ☆   ☆   ☆   ☆   ☆

"MASTER-MINDING"

BACK in the days when Buck Bailey, line coach of Washington State, was still going to college, he played baseball one summer at Brady, Texas. The manager of the team was a former big league pitcher, Bert Maxwell, and the youthful Bailey had implicit confidence in everything that Maxwell told him.

One day, they were playing Coleman, and Brady was behind, 4 to 2, with the ninth inning coming up.

"Looks bad, doesn't it, coach?" observed Bailey, who always called the manager "coach."

"Not so bad," Maxwell replied. "Atkins will lead off with a single, Bailey Jones will get a hit and that will put two men on base; then you'll come up and hit a home run and that will win the game, 5 to 4."

"That would do it, all right," Bailey agreed.

Atkins, first man up, didn't single but he did draw a base on balls; then Jones slapped out a two-bagger, which placed men on second and third. Bailey strode up to the plate, swinging two bats, discarded one, stepped into the batter's box and met the first pitch squarely on the nose, and the ball sailed over the center field fence.

The two runners scored ahead of the burly catcher, and as he rounded third to jog on in home, Bailey turned and yelled to Maxwell: "Well, coach, it worked, didn't it?"

☆   ☆   ☆   ☆   ☆   ☆   ☆

MAIL-ORDER BRIDE

EVERYBODY in the little town knew and liked Big Mack.

He was a hard-working, thrifty farmer, who was close to 50

years old, a bachelor. And then he decided to get married, so he joined a matrimonial bureau and got into correspondence with a widow up North. At last he proposed (sight unseen), was accepted and sent his bride-to-be her railroad fare.

Everybody in town knew about the mail order romance and, when the train rolled in, the platform was crowded. But nobody got off except a traveling man. The train was about to pull out when, out of the coach up near the baggage car, stepped a negro woman.

She caught sight of Big Mack, ran up to him, threw her arms around him and gave him a kiss.

And he kissed her right back because, you see, Big Mack was colored, too!

☆   ☆   ☆   ☆   ☆   ☆   ☆

"LET JUSTICE BE DONE"

HANK long had been renowned in the West Texas oil fields for two characteristics. One was his strength: though only of average height, he had bull-like shoulders and hands that swung almost to his knees.

The other characteristic was his propensity for "borrowing" things. It is related that an oil well supply house received a shipment of drill stems, which — when the trucks backed up to the freight depot platform — proved to be one short. The manager said nothing but, at the end of the month, billed Hank for "One drill stem" and, very promptly, the oil field contractor paid for the item.

When the East Texas discovery was made, oil men rushed in from every point of the compass. Hank had been a celebrity in West Texas, but he was just one more atom among those seething, swarming thousands.

And when (to coin a phrase) the finger of suspicion pointed in his direction regarding the disappearance of a piece of drilling equipment, the owner did not hesitate to file a charge. The case came up for trial and two men testified that, from a distance, they had watched as Hank picked up a drill bit, carried it to a truck, loaded it on the vehicle, then drove away.

The bit was in the courtroom as Exhibit A — a great chunk of steel, weighing perhaps 500 pounds.

No testimony was offered on behalf of the defense but Hank's attorney, in his argument, ridiculed the story of the two men:

"Who would they have you believe the defendant is? Hercules? Samson? Superman?

"Look at that colossal bit! It would be a physical impossibility for any man, even a giant, to pick it up and walk with it

— yet the State of Texas asks you 12 intelligent, upright, patriotic, liberty-loving jurors to believe that my client, who isn't five feet, eight inches tall, could pick up that monstrous mass of metal, carry it to a truck and load it on, unaided!"

The jury returned very shortly with a verdict of "Not guilty."

Hank turned to his lawyer and, in the silence, his voice carried throughout the room:

"Does that mean I get to keep the bit?"

The startled attorney stammered, "I guess it does."

So Hank picked up the bit and walked out with it.

☆　☆　☆　☆　☆　☆　☆

THE "TERROR OF THE FRONTIER"

BACK in the 1880's, when Fort Worth was a roaring frontier town, Algernon Pillsbury was civilized, as he shaved twice a week, and was despised by all the other men.

One day there came into the Red-Eye Saloon, three of the fiercest-looking desperadoes ever seen, even in Fort Worth. They bristled with beards, bowie knives, six-shooters and profanity.

The three seated themselves at a table and, after two drinks of whiskey, began to condemn Texas and Texans.

The place was crowded but none of us felt called upon to remonstrate. None? did I say. There was one who dared do so. Out from a corner stepped the ordinarily pallid and puny Pillsbury — scarcely recognizable now, for his face was flushed with anger, and his eyes glittered.

He marched up to the table and his full five feet, two towered above the strangers, who paused in the midst of their highly-seasoned remarks.

Pillsbury produced a large silver watch and slowly said:

"You men have trampled upon the noblest sentiments of my bosom by the utterances you have uttered in utter disregard of the truth about my beloved State. I will give you three minutes, — three minutes, gentlemen, to take back your words."

Silence fell upon the assembly, except for the ominous ticking of the watch. A minute passed, two minutes, then the leader of the trio said:

"Sir, our remarks were only in fun and we gladly apologize."

And, hastening to down their glasses of liquor, the three men slunk out, their spurs drooping.

We crowded around to slap the hero on the back. A friend exclaimed, "What would you have done if they had refused to take back what they had said?"

Pillsbury looked from face to face and then he half-whispered, "Boys, I would have extended the time."

Injun Fight on the Llano

"Bob, did I ever tell you about our fight with the Injuns over on the Llano?"

"No," said I. "I never heard of it."

"Well! you see, it was in the last quarter of the moon, (Injuns most always commit their deviltries in the last quarter of the moon) in the year, let me see, yes it was the year 1838 — I know it was in 1838, because that was the year of the great overflow in the Colorado. I mind it well, for Uncle Thomas had nigh onto a hundred head of cattle drowned in the bottoms. You know Uncle Thomas don't you? He was one of the first settlers in this country — came out with Stephen F. Austin, and cut down the first stick of timber where the town of 'Nip and Tuck' now is.

" 'Nip and Tuck' you know is about thirty-five miles below here, and in my opinion is one of the likeliest towns this side of the Brazos. The people of that town, too, are mighty clever and sociable, and I must say there is less friction among 'em than you'll find in most of our cities. Everything goes on quiet and smooth, and take my word for it, 'Nip and Tuck' is going to be (with the exception of 'Buck Snort,' where I 'spose you know I own two lots) the largest city in the State of Texas.

"How queer, Bob, the 'State of Texas' sounds to us old settlers, after hearing it called so long the 'Republic.' Ah! well, I was in favor of annexation myself, but still I can't help wishin' for those 'good old times' agin. Times, to be sure, are prosperous enough now, but then they ain't half so lively as them used to be. Then it was first a bout with the Mexicans, then a bufferlo hunt, then a little scrape with the Injuns, and then a . . ."

"But look here," said I, "what about the fight with the Indians over on the Llano?"

"Ah yes! well you see, as I was sayin', it was the last quarter of the moon of the year 1838, when a party of Injuns came down into the settlement on the north prong of the 'Stinkin' Blue,' and stole every critter they could lay their paws upon (except one they killed) and put off for their wig-wams in the mountains. I suppose they call 'em wig-wams, because they generally have so many scalps hangin' up in 'em, that they look like a wig-maker's shop.

"Well, you see, as the Injuns had left us no horses to ride, some fifteen or twenty of us went over to Johnsing's settlement on 'Big Muddy,' not far from where the town of Doe Bleat now is, and borrowed as many as would mount us tolerably well, and arter that it warn't long afore we were on the trail of the Injuns.

"Did you ever foller a trail, Bob? No, well I can tell you it takes a cute feller to do it, just as sure as you are born. But I've often thought that some men have a 'natural turn' for that sort of thing and some haven't. I've been with some men that couldn't foller a loaded wagon and six yoke of oxen, and then again I've been with others that I raly believe could foller a cut-tailed lizard thro' the thickest break on old Caney. If folks ain't born with a 'natural turn' for trailin', and have what I call 'hog knowledge,' they may live in the woods forever and never know much about it.

"You see, sometimes when you are follerin' Injuns, they will scatter like a flock of partridges, and then come together agin a long way off, and then they'll take into the chaparral, (I suppose they calls 'em chaparral because they cuts up a chap's apparel so wretchedly that nothin' but buckskin and an Injun's hide can stand 'em) ;· well, as I was saying, they'll take into the chaparrals so thick that a lizard can't crawl thro' 'em without leavin' most of his hide stickin' to the thorns. Then agin . . "

"But what," said I, "about the fight with the Indians over on the Llano?"

"Ah, yes, well, you see it was the last quarter . . ."

"Oh, never mind the moon," said I, "and the flood, and Uncle Thomas' cattle, and the other preliminaries."

"Oh, yes! well, as I was sayin', we tuck the trail of the Injuns, and followed it to Snake Creek, which we swum not far from where the town of 'Lick-Skillet' now is; and about ten miles beyond there, we cum to the Llano," — (Thank God for that, says I) — "and the first thing we saw after we riz on the bank on the other side, was about fifty of the yaller devils comin' right down on us, screamin' and yellin' like so many prairie wolves. We lit from our horses and treed immediately; and just as I was drawin' a bead on one of the foremost fellows, seven of the ugliest devils 'my blue eyes ever flashed upon,' with nothin' to kiver their nakedness except great splotches of white and black paint, were pointin' their arrows right plum at me" . . . he paused.

"Good gracious! if yonder ain't those plaguey cattle right into the truck patch agin, as sure as shootin'," and off he went right after them at a 2:40 lick; and to this day, this is all I ever heard about his "fight with the Injuns over on the Llano!"

COLONEL GOODNIGHT, the pioneer Panhandle ranchman, was noted for the directness of his speech. An early day preacher was having dinner at the Goodnight home and the rancher's wife asked:

"Where are you from?"

He replied, "I'm from Oklahoma."

"Dern pore recommendation," rumbled Goodnight.

☆　☆　☆　☆　☆　☆　☆

IN THE roaring town of Tascosa, which was the "Cowboy Capital of the Plains" 60 years or more ago, a big, black-mustached newcomer seemed to think it was his "night to howl," and he was doing considerable boasting at the bar. At last he bellowed, "I'm a son-of-a-gun from Kansas."

A cowboy said, "I knew you was a son-of-a-gun, but I didn't know where you was from."

Final Roundup

A SERGEANT was getting a shave and the barber asked, "Haven't I shaved you before?" The veteran replied, "No, I got that scar at Pearl Harbor."

☆　☆　☆　☆　☆　☆　☆

GREENVILLE ("blackest land and whitest people") claims its soil is so rich that when a housewife throws shelled corn to the chickens, they have to catch it on the fly or eat it off the stalk.

☆　☆　☆　☆　☆　☆　☆

THE hotel guest had just paid his bill and he asked, "Do you invite suggestions from your patrons?" "Why, yes," replied the assistant manager. The patron said:

"There is a sign in my room which reads, 'Have you left anything?' I suggest you change it to read, 'Have you anything left?' "

EAST TEXAS: a land of hills, rills, thrills and stills.

☆　☆　☆　☆　☆　☆　☆

THE guest in the Rice Hotel in Houston asked the bellboy who had brought up his baggage, "What's your name?"

The bellboy replied, "Ford."

"What's your first name?"

"Henry."

"Henry Ford," the guest said. "That's a well-known name."

"It ought to be; I been bellhoppin' in this hotel for five years."

☆　☆　☆　☆　☆　☆　☆

TWO MEMBERS of the U.S.N. were chatting in a cafe in Corpus Christi.

"What are you going to do after the war?" one inquired.

The other said, "I'm going to put an oar on my shoulder and start walking inland, and when I come to a place where somebody asks, 'What is that thing you're carrying?' — why, I'm going to settle down right there."

☆　☆　☆　☆　☆　☆　☆

UP IN Missouri, two men were talking and one mentioned "habeas corpus."

"What's that?" the other wanted to know.

"Why, habeas corpus is a seaport in Texas," his friend replied.

☆　☆　☆　☆　☆　☆　☆

THE fishermen were forced ashore during a storm. It was on long and narrow, wild and desolate Padre Island.

"Gee, I sure am hungry," one said.

His companion looked around and remarked, "With all this sand, there must be some spinach."

☆　☆　☆　☆　☆　☆　☆

THE ancient mariner was relating one of his adventures to a group of tourists in Galveston. "A shark grabbed my arm," he said.

"What did you do?" one of the tourists asked.

"I let him have it; I never argue with sharks," he replied.

☆　☆　☆　☆　☆　☆　☆

A COLLEGE MAN is one who can see a pretty ankle three blocks away, while driving an automobile in a crowded street, but will fail to notice, in the wide-open country, the approach of a locomotive the size of a schoolhouse, accompanied by a flock of fifty box cars.

☆　☆　☆　☆　☆　☆　☆

SAN ANTONIO has been called "the most interesting foreign city in the United States."

THE railroad station that serves Uvalde is a mile or so from the center of town. A traveling man complained to the hack-driver, "Why in the world did they build the depot so far from town?" The old fellow drawled, "I dunno, unless it was because they wanted it close to the railroad."

☆　☆　☆　☆　☆　☆　☆

SING while you drive.

At 45 miles an hour, sing "Highways Are Happy Ways"; at 55, "I'm But a Stranger Here—Heaven Is My Home"; at 65, "Nearer, My God, to Thee"; at 75, "When the Roll Is Called Up Yonder, I'll Be There" and, at 85 miles an hour, sing "Lord, I'm Coming Home."

☆　☆　☆　☆　☆　☆　☆

THE old lady asked the brakeman:

"Have we come to Marshall?"

He said, "No — it's a good ways yet."

A few minutes later, he came back through the coach and again she asked him. This kept up until at last he said:

"Madam, if you just won't ask me any more, I'll be sure to let you know when we get there."

So she dozed off, and it was an hour later that she awoke and asked the brakeman:

"Young man, have we come to Marshall yet?"

"Good heavens!" he exclaimed, "we left there 10 minutes ago." So he grabbed the bell-cord, stopped the train and backed it up for six miles.

"All right," he said, "this is where you get off."

"Oh," she said, "I don't want to get off here; my son just told me to be sure and take a dose of my medicine when we got to Marshall."

☆　☆　☆　☆　☆　☆　☆

A TEXAS business man wrote this last will and testament:

"I bequeath to my wife my overdraft at the bank — she can explain it.

"The equity in my car goes to my son — he will then have to go to work to keep up the payments.

"My equipment, give to the junk man — he has had his eye on it for some time.

"I want six of my creditors for pallbearers — they have carried me so long they might as well finish the job."

☆　☆　☆　☆　☆　☆　☆

A NEWCOMER in the dairy business soon found that cows don't give milk — you have to take it away from them.

A COLLEGE STUDENT wrote:

"Dear Dad, Gue$$ what I need mo$t of all. That'$ right. $end it along. Be$t wihe. Your $on, Tom."

And here's the reply:

"Dear Tom, NOthing ever happens here. We kNOw you like your school. Write us aNOther letter. I have to say goodbye NOw."

☆ ☆ ☆ ☆ ☆ ☆ ☆

A WOMAN in a department store fainted and a crowd gathered. A man said, "Has anybody got some whiskey?"

"I have," another spoke up, and produced a bottle.

The man took a big drink, then handed the bottle back, with the remark:

"Thank you; it always did upset me to see a woman faint."

☆ ☆ ☆ ☆ ☆ ☆ ☆

"WHAT happened at school today?" the fond mother asked.

Little Willie replied, "The teacher asked us where we were born?"

"Did you tell her?"

"Well, I didn't want to say that I was born in a hospital — that would sound like I was a sissy," the boy replied.

"Then, where did you tell her you were born?" his mother asked.

"Oh, I told her I was born in the T.C.U. stadium," he answered.

☆ ☆ ☆ ☆ ☆ ☆ ☆

THE intoxicated young man on the passenger train would alternately sing and talk in a loud tone. A minister surveyed him with disfavor and then said, "Young man, you are bound for h——."

"I don't care," the other replied, "I got a round trip ticket."

☆ ☆ ☆ ☆ ☆ ☆ ☆

OIL FIELD SAYING: "You spud in at the surface and sue at the sand."

☆ ☆ ☆ ☆ ☆ ☆ ☆

A DEALER in leases and royalties wanted to buy a share in a landowner's royalty.

He said, "I'll give you $1,000 for a thirty-second."

"I don't want to sell that much," the farmer replied.

"Well, I'll pay you $500 and take a sixteenth."

"It's a deal," the farmer said.

☆ ☆ ☆ ☆ ☆ ☆ ☆

WOMAN — A person who can hurry through an aisle eighteen inches wide without knocking down piled-up tinware, and then drive home and knock the doors off a twelve-foot garage.

A NEW traveling salesman turned in his expense account and one item was "Overcoat, $25." The manager struck out that item. Next week, when the drummer turned in another expense account, the manager looked it over and then said, "Let me compliment you; you haven't listed an overcoat this time." The traveling man said, "Oh, it's there, all right; you just don't see it."

☆ ☆ ☆ ☆ ☆ ☆ ☆

AN ADULT has been defined as a man who has quit growing, except in the middle.

☆ ☆ ☆ ☆ ☆ ☆ ☆

WHEN the fire alarm sounds, a dangerous character puts in his appearance — the man with the axe—and "Texas Siftings" thus portrays him:

He is always early at a fire, accompanied by a new axe. No 'one knows where he got the axe and no one ever sees him carrying it back to where he got it, but while he is on the ground, he makes things lively. He batters in doors, hacks the fence in a vain effort to cut it away to make room for the engine and, in his wild desire to save property, he demolishes everything that an axe will make an impression on. This fiend, who is too weak to do any manual labor and who lets his wife chop all the firewood at home, will create havoc and destruction for two blocks around a fire.

☆ ☆ ☆ ☆ ☆ ☆ ☆

THE patient stirred, slowly opened one eye, and then the other, and found himself swathed in bandages and encased in casts.

"What on earth happened?" he asked.

A friend at the bedside said, "Don't you remember meeting me and coming up to my room on the third floor of the Texas Hotel, and we had a drink and then another one?"

"Yes, I remember that."

"And then two friends came in and we had two more drinks."

"Yes, I can remember that, too."

"And then you opened the window, got out on the ledge, crooked your arms, worked them up and down and said, 'I'm a little bird and I'm gonna fly around this building and come back and light in this window'?"

The injured man exclaimed, "Good heavens, did I say that? Why didn't you stop me?"

"Stop you!" his friend echoed. "Why, I bet $25 you could do it!"

☆ ☆ ☆ ☆ ☆ ☆ ☆

AS YOU ENTER a South Texas village, you see this sign: "Drive slow and see our town; drive fast and see our jail."

AND another town has a traffic sign that reads: "Stop — and save $5."

☆　☆　☆　☆　☆　☆　☆

A PARTY of city sportsmen was out on a hunting expedition during the deer season in Mason County. From the woods near the cabin came a cry, "Hello, this is Henry!"

"All right, this is Bill!" one shouted back.

"Bill, are all the other boys there?"

"Yes."

"Is the guide there, too?"

"Yes, he's here."

"Then I've killed a deer."

☆　☆　☆　☆　☆　☆　☆

SOMEONE has said that college education for women is useless — if they're pretty, they don't need it; and if they're not, it's inadequate.

☆　☆　☆　☆　☆　☆　☆

THE bases were full and the count was "two-and-three" on the batter. After the next pitch, the umpire called, "Ball four; you're out."

"What do you mean I'm out?" demanded the batter.

"You're out," the umpire repeated, " 'cause there ain't no place to put you."

☆　☆　☆　☆　☆　☆　☆

IN THE Huntsville prison shops, one of the inmates mumbled to a newcomer, "How long you in for?" The other whispered, "Ten years." The first one looked around cautiously, slipped him a note and murmured, "Mail this for me when you get out."

＼　☆　☆　☆　☆　☆　☆　☆

THE Golden Gloves Tournament was in progress in Fort Worth. In this particular bout, it was soon apparent that one of the boys was no match for the other, but when the battered boxer reeled to his corner at the end of the first round, his second (in accord with the immemorial tradition of seconds) wanted to keep up his fighter's confidence and so he said:

"You're going great; you're a mile ahead."

The next round was even worse than the first, but the boy was game and lasted it out. As he returned to his corner, his second said:

"You're beating him bad; he hasn't laid a glove on you."

Looking up with the one eye that was still partly open, through puffed and bleeding lips, the lad said:

"Then you keep your eye on the referee this next round; some son-of-a-gun is beatin' h—— outta me!"

THE young man and his beautiful companion were late in arriving at the stadium for the Baylor-A. & M. game. As they reached their seats, he asked a fan, "What's the score?"

The spectator replied, "0-0."

"Good, we haven't missed anything," gushed the girl.

☆　☆　☆　☆　☆　☆　☆

JONES took up fishing and, like all fishermen, he enjoyed telling about the dimension of the various fish that he landed. His friends questioned his veracity — or, to put it in plain English, they implied he was a durn liar.

So he bought a pair of scales, installed them at his home and would weigh each fish and, thereby, have proof to back up his claims.

All went well until one day a young man who lived next door came over, excited, and said:

"I want to borrow those scales."

In a little while, the neighbor returned, still more excited, and said:

"Congratulate me — congratulate me; I'm the new father of a 64-pound baby boy!"

☆　☆　☆　☆　☆　☆　☆

IT was late at night, but the out-of-town visitor decided that maybe he could get shelter at the home of a friend, all the hotels being full.

He was not sure of the address, and after he had knocked on the door several times, a woman's voice was heard:

"What is it?"

"Does Henry Green live here?"

"Yes," she replied, "bring him in."

☆　☆　☆　☆　☆　☆　☆

FOR MANY YEARS, there was a colored barber in Austin with a shop near the Capitol, and many of the State's officials were his customers.

One day, a new Senator entered for a shave and as he reclined in the chair, the old barber said:

"Suh, you reminds me ob General Sam Houston."

The statesman smiled and said, "Is it my broad brow?"

"Naw, suh."

"My stalwart physique then?"

" 'Taint dat, neither, suh."

"My voice, then?"

"Naw, suh, it's yore breath."

"My breath?" the Senator repeated, perplexedly.

"Yas, suh; you drinks de same brand ob whiskey," the old "uncle" replied.

WHEN old Sam was president of the Texas Republic, he received a challenge to fight a duel with a man whom he considered his inferior.

Addressing the bearer of the challenge, he said:

"Sir, tell your principal that Sam Houston never fights down hill!"

☆ ☆ ☆ ☆ ☆ ☆ ☆

THE man who declares, "I run things at my house," probably means the lawn-mower, washing machine, baby carriage and errands.

☆ ☆ ☆ ☆ ☆ ☆ ☆

PERKINS had fallen and injured his arm severely.

"How long will it be before I can play the piano?" he asked.

"Oh, about a month," the doctor replied.

"That's fine; I never could play it before."

☆ ☆ ☆ ☆ ☆ ☆ ☆

AND there was another man who was asked, "Can you play the piano?" and he answered, "I don't know; I never tried."

☆ ☆ ☆ ☆ ☆. ☆ ☆

THE minister was speaking on "The Minor Prophets." He had been talking for over an hour and had not yet concluded.

"And now," he shouted, "there is Malachi; where shall we place Malachi?"

A man arose and said, "He can have my place; I'm leaving."

☆ ☆ ☆ ☆ ☆ ☆ ☆

A SOLDIER from the Lone Star State wrote back from overseas, "The durn fellers in my outfit have rationed the number of times a day that I can say 'Texas'."

☆ ☆ ☆ ☆ ☆ ☆ ☆

AN El Paso policeman brought in a prisoner. "What charge?" asked the desk sergeant.

"I don't exactly know."

"Well, what did he do?"

The arresting officer replied, "He knocked at the side-door of a tavern, and the bartender pushed the door open a little and shoved out a glass of whiskey."

The sergeant wrote:

"Impersonating an officer."

☆ ☆ ☆ ☆ ☆ ☆ ☆

A SOUTH TEXAS RANCHER, suddenly rich from oil, had built a fine home, and the members of the family were planning the furnishings. A son said, "We ought to have a chandelier in the library."

The ranchman said, "All right, but I'll bet there ain't anybody in this family who can play the durn thing."

THE town drunkard was also its most widely-read man. He was attending a revival and, when the evangelist completed a resounding passage, the listener said in a voice that could be heard throughout the tent:

"That's Dwight L. Moody."

The preacher ignored the remark and, when he had rolled out another brilliant passage, the listener commented:

"That's Billy Sunday."

But when a third utterance drew the remark, "That's Henry Ward Beecher," the evangelist angrily exclaimed:

"You're a confounded fool!"

To which the scholar replied, "That's original."

☆　☆　☆　☆　☆　☆　☆

ASSOCIATE JUSTICE MILBURN LONG of the Eastland Court of Civil Appeals tells of a colorful West Texas lawyer who had a friend who dealt in odd lots of merchandise, and on one occasion bought a bankrupt stock of drugs. A flood swept through the building where the stock was stored and washed all the labels off the bottles.

The old lawyer remarked, "Bill, you are really in a h—— of a shape; you don't know whether you drink it or rub it on."

☆　☆　☆　☆　☆　☆　☆

JONES was good and mad because a bill was long over-due and he dictated a letter to the debtor:

"My secretary is a lady and I am a gentleman, so I can not tell you what you are; but you, being neither, will know what I mean."

☆　☆　☆　☆　☆　☆　☆

WHEN Henry Helms, leader of the Santa Claus bank robbers, was in jail at Eastland awaiting the trial which sent him to the electric chair, a well-meaning social worker visited the jail and said:

"I hope you men are leading an upright life."

"Well, ma'am," Helms replied, "we ain't stayin' out late at night."

☆　☆　☆　☆　☆　☆　☆

TEXAS of course leads in athletics.

For instance, there is a runner who is so fast he can beat his voice to the top of El Capitan peak, admire the view for half an hour and then catch up with his echo.

He went by a coyote so fast that he mistook the animal for a century plant — and when he ran from Texline to Laredo, he started slowing down just past San Antonio so as not to wind up across in Old Mexico, as he had not provided himself with a passport.

A FEW SIGNS in taverns:

Don't swear before ladies; let them swear first.

Mary had a little lamb; what will you have?

No checks cashed; we have agreed to stay out of the banking business if the bank will stay out of the cafe business.

You don't have to be crazy to tend bar but it helps a lot.

Checks cashed only for men above 90 years of age and when accompanied by both parents.

☆ ☆ ☆ ☆ ☆ ☆ ☆

THERE had been a cloudburst during the night, and the water rose so rapidly that the family took refuge in the attic. As the father looked out next morning, he saw a straw hat float across the front yard and then back, then across once more.

"What in the world!" he exclaimed.

"Oh, that's Uncle Elmer," one of the boys explained. "He swore he was gonna mow the lawn today, come h— or high water!"

☆ ☆ ☆ ☆ ☆ ☆ ☆

HE was the county's richest man — and one of the reasons was that he never paid a bill if he could get out of doing so. One night, he partook copiously and was sleeping late next morning when there came a knock on the door. He mumbled, "Sue and be d——d," and rolled over and went back to sleep.

☆ ☆ ☆ ☆ ☆ ☆ ☆

SIGN in a cafe:

"We'll sympathize with you if your wife doesn't understand you; we'll hold your horse: we'll tend to your baby — but don't ask us to cash your check."

☆ ☆ ☆ ★ ☆ ☆ ☆

WHEN Billy Rose was planning the glamorous spectacle, the Fort Worth Casa Manana, which was to establish him as the greatest showman of this generation, many performers called on him in an effort to be included in the show. Among them was a crank who said, "For a thousand dollars, I will commit suicide on the stage in full view of the audience."

Rose said, "That's fine — but what would you do for an encore?"

☆ ☆ ☆ ☆ ☆ ☆ ☆

TEXANS have changed Emerson's saying a little — they hitch their wagon to the Lone Star.

☆ ☆ ☆ ☆ ☆ ☆ ☆

TEXAS is so vast that, in early days when travel was primitive, there was one instance of a baby that was born in Texarkana and, by the time the covered wagon reached El Paso, he was rolling his own cigarettes.

WHEN the railroad was built into Rising Star and the first train arrived, the strange sight was greeted by the entire population. Suddenly, the engineer thrust his head out of the cab window and yelled, "Look out, folks,· I'm going to turn the engine around!" and there was the greatest scatteration ever seen in Eastland County.

☆   ☆   ☆   ☆   ☆   ☆   ☆

AND speaking of Rising Star, the proprietor of the novelty store is W. J. Herrington, former county official and the possessor of a sense of humor. During the depression, there was a parade for the opening of the Free Fall Fair, and Bill drove a buggy, on which there was a sign, "Our store sells no goods on Sunday — and very little the rest of the week!"

☆   ☆   ☆   ☆   ☆   ☆   ☆

A BARBER was shaving a hollow-cheeked man and, to round out the sunken face, thrust his finger inside his customer's mouth. The razor slipped, cut completely through the man's cheek and nicked the barber's finger. He yelled, "You lantern-jawed son-of-a-gun, see what you made me do to my finger!"

☆   ☆   ☆   ☆   ☆   ☆   ☆

A ROAD SIGN:
  "This is God's country; don't drive through it like h——."

☆   ☆   ☆   ☆   ☆   ☆   ☆

"MY big brother is the star dash man of Port Arthur," said one small boy to another. "My, he's so fast that he can switch off the electric light in the middle of the room and be in bed before the room gets dark."

☆   ☆   ☆   ☆   ☆   ☆   ☆

AND that was nearly as good as the boxer who was so shifty that he could get under a shower bath and stay there for half an hour with the shower turned on full blast and yet never get hit by a drop.

☆   ☆   ☆   ☆   ☆   ☆   ☆

THE tendency of Texans to observe almost any occasion with a barbecue caused George Sessions Perry to comment, "In Texas, we barbecue anything that will stand still."

☆   ☆   ☆   ☆   ☆   ☆   ☆

A SOLDIER, who had been training in Texas and so of course had heard from the natives about its countless glories, was visiting the folks back home. A friend said, "Tell us about Texas — is it a State?"
  "No," the soldier replied, "it's a state of mind."

THE fortune-teller gazed into the crystal ball and then said, "Mr. Doakes, you will be poor for the next ten years."

"Yes," he questioned eagerly, "and then?"

"Oh, by that time, you'll be used to it," she replied.

☆ ☆ ☆ ☆ ☆ ☆ ☆

THE patient was poor in both purse and physique. He called on a doctor who felt his pulse, looked at his tongue and peered into his eyes, then said:

"I'll examine you for $10."

"Good," said the man, "and if you find it, I want half."

☆ ☆ ☆ ☆ ☆ ☆ ☆

THESE are supposed to be actual quotations turned in to State headquarters in Austin by social workers:

"These people are extremely cultured; something should be done about their condition immediately."

"Family's savings all used up — relatives have helped."

"Woman says husband has illness that sounds like arithmetic. I think she means arthritis."

"Man hit by automobile — speaks broken English."

☆ ☆ ☆ ☆ ☆ ☆ ☆

MAN criticizes woman for her extravagance — but she never wastes a dollar's worth of shotgun shells to get one dove; nor goes into restaurant and buys a thirty-five cent meal and gives the waitress a twenty-five cent tip because she smiles at him; nor buys a dollar's worth of minnows to catch one poor little fish.

☆ ☆ ☆ ☆ ☆ ☆ ☆

JONES liked to play poker and every Saturday night he would hurry over to the hotel, as soon as he had drawn his pay, for a session. He was playing with a bunch of "sharks" and he never won. This particular Saturday night, when he knocked on the door of the hotel room, there was no response. So he chunked his week's salary through the transom and remarked to himself, "They'd a-got it, anyhow."

☆ ☆ ☆ ☆ ☆ ☆ ☆

TEXAS uses Spanish land measurements. A "vara" has been defined as the distance a Mexican could travel while smoking a cigarette aboard a burro. (A "vara" is less than three feet.)

☆ ☆ ☆ ☆ ☆ ☆ ☆

THE meanest man in Texas?

Maybe he was the Corsicana citizen who announced, "I'm going home and if my wife don't have dinner ready, I'm going to raise thunder; and if she does have it ready, I'm not going to eat a bite."

OR IT might have been the Sweetwater man with a hang-over, who kicked the cat out of the parlor, and remarked: "Come in here and stomp around, will you?"

☆ ☆ ☆ ☆ ☆ ☆ ☆

STILL, it could have been the man in McAllen who gave his little boy a nickel for taking a dose of bad-tasting medicine just before going to bed — then slipped up, while his son was asleep, and took the money back — and next morning whipped him for losing it.

And, as if that weren't mean enough, the father took all those nickels and, when the medicine was all gone, used the money to buy another bottle!

☆ ☆ ☆ ☆ ☆ ☆ ☆

STILL speaking of "the meanest man," there was the father in Fort Worth and his little boy came in all out of breath and said, proudly, "I followed a street car all the way home from town and saved 8⅓ cents" — and the father gave him a whipping because he hadn't followed a bus home and saved a dime!

☆ ☆ ☆ ☆ ☆ ☆ ☆

IT was a Scotchman, however, and not a Texas resident who, two nights before Christmas, went out behind the barn, fired a shot, then came in and told the children that Santa Claus had committed suicide!

☆ ☆ ☆ ☆ ☆ ☆ ☆

STREET CAR FARE in Austin was a nickel and there was talk of raising it to a dime.

One citizen remarked, "I don't care; I never ride the street car, anyhow; I walk and save my money — so if they raise the fare to a dime, I'll get rich twice as quick."

☆ ☆ ☆ ☆ ☆ ☆ ☆

A WOMAN got on a city bus in Houston and a man arose and offered her a seat. She fainted.

When she was revived, she thanked him — and the man fainted!

☆ ☆ ☆ ☆ ☆ ☆ ☆

THE president of a bank was talking to the chairman of the board. He said, "Brown has been with us 20 years; we will either have to raise his salary $10 a month or make him a vice president."

☆ ☆ ☆ ☆ ☆ ☆ ☆

THE evangelist delivered a stirring sermon on prohibition, concluding with, "My friends, would that all the whiskey in Tyler were poured into the Neches River!"

Then he announced, "The congregation will now rise and sing, 'Shall We Gather at the River?'"

A LONG DISTANCE CALL came through from New York for a man in Lamesa. There was no answer at home so the Lamesa operator said, "He may have left for the gin," so she rang there, but he was not there, either, she reported.

"Well," said the New York operator, "are there any other saloons you could try?"

☆ ☆ ☆ ☆ ☆ ☆ ☆

THE doctor explained to Higgins that he had a serious ailment for which an operation was absolutely necessary.

The patient turned pale and asked, "Isn't it very dangerous?"

"Yes," the doctor said, "five out of six who undergo this operation die, but you have nothing to worry about — you are a cinch to recover because my last five patients died."

☆ ☆ ☆ ☆ ☆ ☆ ☆

SIMILAR but different is the story of the eminent surgeon who lectured in medical college. He took his class through the hospital and, at the first room, he described the patient's symptoms, and then asked the first student, "Brown, would you operate?" Brown hesitated, then slowly replied, "No, I don't believe I would."

"Smith, what about you?" the surgeon asked.

The next student followed the lead of the first one and said he would not operate. The same view was expressed by the other four students.

"You are all wrong," the surgeon said, briskly. "I'm going to operate in half an hour."

The patient, who up until now had been silent, spoke up:

"The h—— you are! I'm a good Democrat; six-to-one is enough of a majority for me; gimme my pants — I'm going home!"

☆ ☆ ☆ ☆ ☆ ☆ ☆

ELMER was not drunk, you understand. He'd had seven or six drinks and he was a little glassy-eyed and thick of speech, but he wasn't drunk — and he was hungry.

So he entered a cafe, seated himself at a table and when he looked up, he saw a waitress standing there. Elmer said, "I want somethin' to eat — don't care what it is — but am in hurry."

"Yes, sir," she replied.

Now this waitress was unfortunate in that she had legs of unequal length. She was standing on the longer leg and when she took a step and dropped down in height, Elmer called out, "Hold on, if you have to go down in the cellar for it, I haven't got time to wait."

THE annual banquet of the Chamber of Commerce was in progress and the master of ceremonies called upon a school teacher to respond to the toast, "Long live our teachers!"

The response in full was, "On what?"

☆　☆　☆　☆　☆　☆　☆

"LEMME have a dime fer somethin' to eat," the tramp whined.

The citizen ran his hand in his pocket, but a thought hit him and he inquired, "Do you drink anything?"

The panhandler's face brightened as he answered, "Yes — anything."

☆　☆　☆　☆　☆　☆　☆

THE early-day color of San Antonio is depicted by Frank Bushick the historian: "The yelping of the coyotes mingled with the reverberations of the vesper bells. Game of all sorts was plentiful — including monte, poker and seven up."

☆　☆　☆　☆　☆　☆　☆

AT LAST, the town's old maid was going to be married and she was talking over the plans for the ceremony. The minister asked, "I suppose you want the organist to play the Wedding March as you come down the aisle?"

She said, "No, I think it would be more appropriate to play that old hymn, 'This Is the Way I Long Have Sought and Mourned Because I Found It Not.'"

☆　☆　☆　☆　☆　☆　☆

ELOQUENTLY, the preacher preached — likewise long. After an hour and a half, he reached the climax:

"Brethren and sisters, on that final day when the trumpet shall sound, the sky will roll up like a scroll; the mountains will tumble; the lightnings will flash; the lakes, the rivers and the seas will dry up — but I never will!"

☆　☆　☆　☆　☆　☆　☆

SIGN in a Tyler cafe, "Our food is like mother used to cook before she took up bridge."

☆　☆　☆　☆　☆　☆　☆

THE telephone rang and the night manager of the hotel answered.

"This is Brown in 818 and I want the house physician right away," said a fuzzy voice.

The manager asked, "Are you sick?"

"No, it's my friend, Bill."

Suspecting that he was dealing with a case of intoxication, the hotel man inquired, "Is he seeing things?"

"No," said Brown, "that's just it: the room is full of things crawling and running around and he can't see a one!"

BACK in prohibition days, an old soak remarked: "The feller who named near-beer was a durn poor judge of distance."

☆ ☆ ☆ ☆ ☆ ☆ ☆

THE banker was the richest member of the little town's congregation and so, when the minister told of the need of money with which to repair the church, everyone waited for Banker Smith to lead off the subscriptions.

He said, "I'll give $5."

Just then, a chunk of plaster fell and hit him on the head.

He said, hastily: "I mean $25."

A brother in the "amen corner" said:

"Oh, Lord, hit him again."

☆ ☆ ☆ ☆ ☆ ☆ ☆

A VILLAGER claimed that he had beheld a vision summoning him to the ministry. He had seen, he said, two giant clouds in the form of the letters, "G P," meaning "Go preach." After hearing several of his efforts in the pulpit, the church board called him in and the spokesman said, "Brother, we don't doubt that you saw the vision; you just misinterpreted it. That 'G P' meant 'Go plow.'"

☆ ☆ ☆ ☆ ☆ ☆ ☆

LITTLE JOHNNY lived in Comanche County where there are no negroes. Visiting his uncle in Fort Worth, the lad was taken for a stroll through Burnet Park, in the center of the city, and he saw the first colored person he had ever seen — a large negress.

"Uncle," he said, excitedly, "that woman's face is black."

"Yes," the uncle replied.

"And her hand is black."

"Yes, yes."

"And her arms are black, too."

"Yes, she's black all over."

The boy looked up into his uncle's face admiringly and said, "Uncle, you know everything, don't you?"

☆ ☆ ☆ ☆ ☆ ☆ ☆

GENERALLY SPEAKING, women are — generally speaking.

☆ ☆ ☆ ☆ ☆ ☆

SHANGHAI PIERCE affectionately called his longhorns "sea-lions." The hardy breed flourished even in the marshlands, using their great horns to swing from limb to limb of trees, with the agility of monkeys, in getting over the worst spots.

The flesh of such cattle was what one would imagine. In fact it is recorded that a boatload of the "sea-lions" was shipped to the Spanish army in Cuba, and the commanding officer cabled, "Send no more of such cattle; one more boatload and the entire army will rise in revolt."

THE Rev. Perry Gresham, former Fort Worth minister, was introduced to an audience as Dr. Gresham soon after he had received a high degree. Modestly, he said:

"There is considerable misunderstanding about the real meaning of the various degrees. M.D. means 'moderately dumb'; D.D. means 'decidedly dumb'; and Ph.D. means 'phenomenally dumb.'"

☆　☆　☆　☆　☆　☆　☆

THE teacher was conducting an arithmetic lesson. "Willie," she asked, "if coal is $5 a ton and your father buys $30 worth, how much will he get?"

"Five tons," the pupil replied.

The instructor said, "But that's not right!"

"I know it isn't," the boy said, "but that's the way they do you."

☆　☆　☆　☆　☆　☆　☆

"WHAT is the best way to keep milk from souring?" a subscriber wrote in, and the editor at Muleshoe replied, "Leave it in the cow."

☆　☆　☆　☆　☆　☆　☆

A SUCCESSFUL OIL MAN was asked, "Did you have much capital when you started?" He said, "Why I had so little that I took leases miles and miles from production, and the consideration was 'one dollar and other valuable consideration,' and if the farmer insisted on actually receiving the dollar, I wouldn't take the lease because I'd have been out of capital!"

☆　☆　☆　☆　☆　☆　☆

THE lads were boasting about their fathers' wealth.

"My father is worth $50,000," said one.

"Mine is worth a hundred thousand," said another.

The third boy was silent a while and then he remarked, "My father is worth $5,000 in Georgia."

"What do you mean — in Georgia?" the others demanded.

"That's what the sheriff offers for him."

☆　☆　☆　☆　☆　☆　☆

As Hick Halcomb used to say:

There are three planks in my platform —

        1. I love my friends.
        2. I love my friends.
        3. I love my friends.

The End

CPSIA information can be obtained
at www.ICGtesting.com
Printed in the USA
LVOW10s0309130617

537815LV00002B/381/P